With

Dickens

at

Christmas

Stephen Poxon is a writer, editor and compiler of devotional works. He compiled A Pleasant Year with Father Brown: 365 daily readings in the company of G. K. Chesterton's priest detective *(Darton, Longman and Todd, 2022). His other 'Through the Year' books include as subjects Catherine Booth, William Booth, John Wesley, Charles Wesley, and John Newton.*

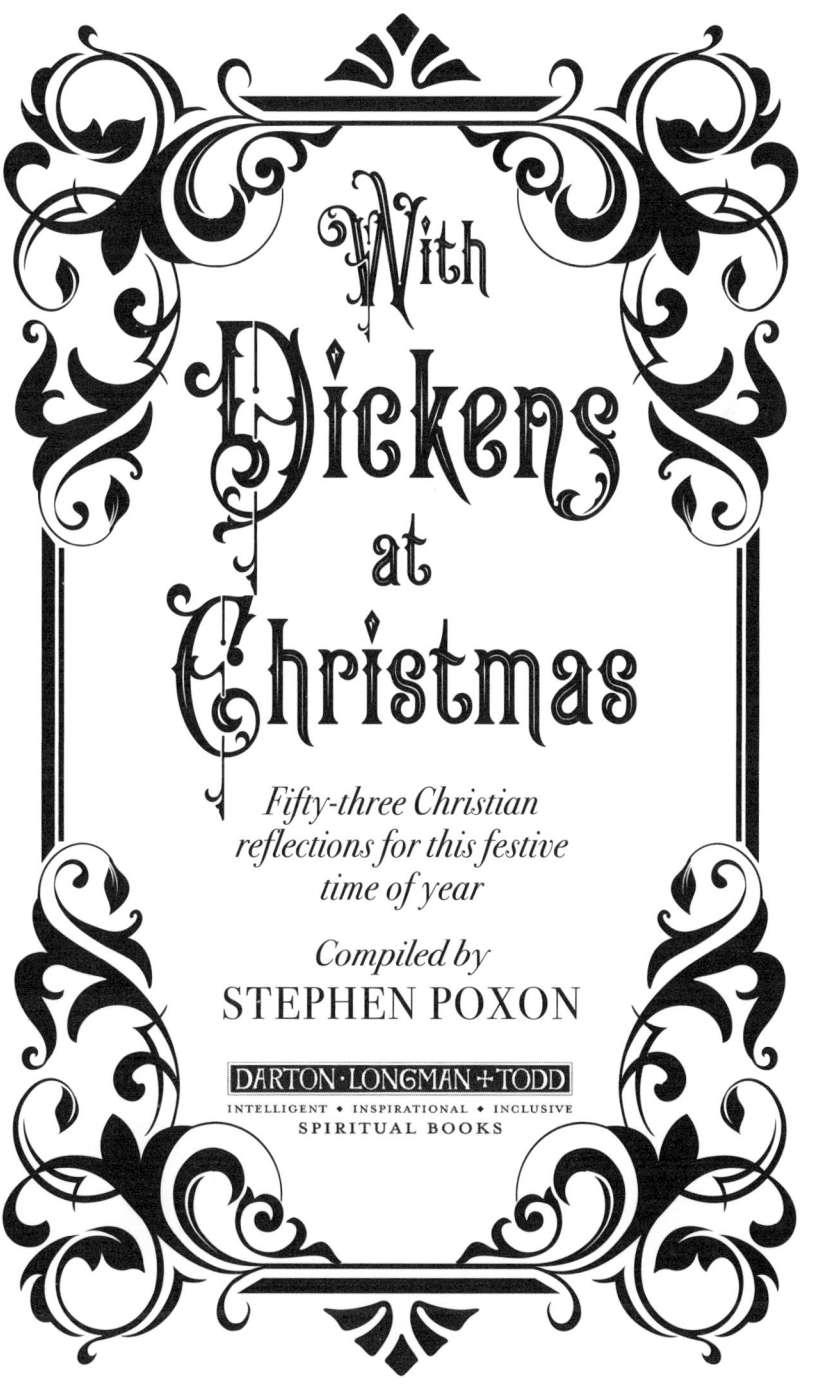

With
Dickens
at
Christmas

*Fifty-three Christian
reflections for this festive
time of year*

Compiled by
STEPHEN POXON

DARTON · LONGMAN + TODD
INTELLIGENT ◆ INSPIRATIONAL ◆ INCLUSIVE
SPIRITUAL BOOKS

First published in 2025 by
Darton, Longman and Todd Ltd
Unit 1, The Exchange
6 Scarbrook Road
Croydon CR0 1UH
editorial@darton-longman-todd.co.uk

This product conforms to the requirements of the European Union's General
Product Safety Regulations (GPSR).
EU Authorised Representative for GPSR:
Easy Access System Europe –
Mustamäe tee 50, 10621 Tallinn, Estonia
gpsr.requests@easproject.com

Illustrations from Michael John Goodman, Charles Dickens Illustrated Gallery,
www.CharlesDickensIllustration.org

ISBN: 978-1-915412-85-0

A catalogue record for this book is available from the British Library.

Printed and bound in India by Replika Press Pvt. Ltd.

Introduction

It is often said, or at least imagined, that Charles Dickens invented Christmas. While this is clearly not the case, since Christmas has been celebrated for over two thousand years, long before Dickens was born in 1812, it is not inaccurate to say that Dickens reinvented the season. With the release of his 1843 novella *A Christmas Carol*, he reshaped how we understand Christmas.

At the heart of the story is the profound transformation of Ebenezer Scrooge, a miser who initially sees Christmas as a pointless drain on time and money. His journey from greed to generosity mirrors the decline and revival of the Christmas spirit itself.

In this sense, Dickens did more than capture the essence of Christmas in *A Christmas Carol*; he helped to revive it in the cultural imagination. Nearly two centuries after its publication, the novella remains as relevant as ever, offering a message that cuts through materialism and commercial hustle. By following Scrooge's whimsical yet life-changing adventures, readers are reminded of the true heart of Christmas.

The enduring influence of *A Christmas Carol* across generations highlights its lasting impact: a story that connects personal struggles with the universal hope for transformation and redemption.

Dickens described the Christmas holiday as 'a good time: a

kind, forgiving, charitable, pleasant time: the only time I know of in the long calendar of the year, when men and women seem by one consent to open their shut-up hearts freely, and to think of other people below them as if they really were fellow-passengers to the grave, and not another race of creatures bound on other journeys' (*A Christmas Carol*).

Without exaggeration or overstatement, then, it could be argued that Charles Dickens has had more influence on how we traditionally celebrate Christmas today than any other individual in history – except one, that is, the central character of the seasonal narrative, Our Lord himself; the Christ whose Mass is fundamental to everything else that might take place.

This book, it should be noted, is not by any means a biography of the man, and neither is it an academic exploration of Dickens' works. It does not pretend to be, and should not be read in that light. It is entirely, and only, a devotional work, written and edited with one intention in mind; that of offering readers devotional access to some of the glories and wonders of the special seasons of Advent, Christmas, and New Year.

Charles Dickens wrote a number of Christmas stories and books, some of which have been plundered and part-excavated here. Whilst not every story of his addresses Christmas specifically, the recurring themes of what has been referred to as his 'carol philosophy' should be evident throughout, and can be detected 'between the lines', as it were; goodwill, spiritual reflection, our common humanity, and, sometimes, reverence and worship. Those strands mingle and mix within the excerpts chosen here.

Second-to-none as a genial master of observational writing, Dickens repeatedly and ingeniously highlights the amusing, the frightening, the dangerous and the endearing as human traits, qualities and flaws common to one and all, and in doing so, subtly brings to mind all that Christmas is, essentially, all about;

namely, helpless humankind in dire need of a Saviour – in this case, a baby within whose nature was gift-wrapped, in swaddling cloths, the entirety of God.

Readers should perhaps be aware of the danger of looking for a coherent sequence dealing with Advent, Christmas, and New Year, in that particular calendar order. That search will lead to disappointment. Rather, the better beauty of these pages can be found (experienced, sensed) if those seasons are relaxed from their strictest definitions and allowed to merge as one glorious, astonishing story, that of Jesus Christ coming to us as God incarnate, in a lowly manger. The richness of Charles Dickens' words, married to verses of Scripture, extracts from Christmas carols, and meditations, should all combine to gently provoke prayer and personal devotional consideration.

My warmest thanks are extended to everyone at Darton, Longman and Todd who has helped to facilitate this lovely opportunity. I regard it as a great privilege to be involved in this project, and I am most grateful to have received lots of help along the way. Likewise, thanks, as always, to my family, for their typically unfailing encouragement and support. Another portion of my sincere gratitude is extended to my friend Reverend Fraser Penny, Minister of Dunkeld Parish Church and Cathedral, whose initial suggestion sparked this whole idea. (Who would have imagined the impact an off-the-cuff remark made after a church service might make? Certainly not me.)

My prayer is that every reader will experience something of the love and Lordship of Christ through these thoughts and ponderings. We are each stepping into a narrative that is already centuries old, as witnessed by some of the carols referred to in these daily readings. Within that context, whereby ancient counsel stands helpfully alongside present concerns, I hope this modest offering serves to enrich Advent, Christmas, and New Year for many.

> This King is come to save his kind,
> In the scripture as we find;
> Therefore this song we have in mind:
> In excelsis gloria.[1]

> *'I will honour Christmas in my heart,*
> *and try to keep it all the year.'* [2]

SJP
Hertfordshire, 2024

---

[1] From the carol *In excelsis gloria*, written in 1456. Authorship uncertain.
[2] Charles Dickens, *A Christmas Carol*.

With Dickens at Christmas

Reflections

**She gave birth to her firstborn, a son. She wrapped
him in cloths and placed him in a manger, because
there was no guest room available for them.
(Luke 2:7 NIV)**

There are not many people – and it is desirable that a story-teller and a story-reader should establish a mutual understanding as soon as possible, I beg it to be noticed that I confine this observation neither to young people not to little people, but extend it to all conditions of people: little and big, young and old: yet growing up, or already growing down again – there are not, I say, many people who would care to sleep in a church. I don't mean at sermon-time in warm weather (when the thing has actually been done, once or twice), but in the night, and alone. A great multitude of persons will be violently astonished, I know, by this position, in the broad bold day. But it applies to night. It must be argued, and I will undertake to maintain it successfully on any gusty winter's night appointed for the purpose, with any one opponent chosen from the rest, who will meet me singly in an old churchyard, before an old church door; and will previously empower me to lock him in, if needful to his satisfaction, until morning. For the night wind has a dismal trick of wandering round and round a building of that sort, and moaning as it goes; and of trying, with its unseen hand, the windows and the doors; and seeking out some crevices by which to enter. And when it has got in; as one not finding what it seeks, whatever that may be, it wails and howls to issue forth again: and not content with stalking through the aisles, and gliding round and round the pillars, and tempting the deep organ, soars up to the roof, and strives to rend the rafters: then flings itself despairingly upon the stones below, and passes, muttering, into the vaults. Anon, it comes up stealthily, and creeps along the walls, seeming to read, in whispers, the inscriptions sacred to the dead. At some of these, it breaks out shrilly, as with laughter; and at others, moans and cries as if it were lamenting. It has a ghostly sound too, lingering within the altar; where it seems to chant, in its wild way, of wrong and murder done, and false gods worshipped, in defiance of the tables of the Law, which look so fair and smooth, but are so flawed and broken. Ugh! Heaven preserve us, sitting snugly round the fire! It has an awful voice, that wind at midnight, singing in a church![3]

Warm-hearted God, how utterly dreadful it must be, perhaps especially throughout the bleak midwinter, to have nowhere to sleep except on a pavement or in a shop doorway: bitterly cold, lonely, frightening, dehumanising, and depressing. Even trying to sleep in an empty, freezing church would be preferable. Lord, I pray for churches and charities whose doors will be open during this season, where a friendly welcome to rough sleepers is guaranteed, and maybe the provision of hot food too. Bless all such endeavours.

No room in the inn for the travellers weary,
Though hungry and thirsty and footsore they be;
The children of David, in David's own city,
They come to enrol at the Caesar's decree.
No place but the stable for Joseph and Mary,
Although they are own'd of the true royal line;
They turn from the inn, from its warmth and its plenty,
To rest for the night with the asses and kine.[4] [5]

[3] *The Chimes.*

[4] Archaic word for cows or cattle.

[5] From a carol of the same name by Reverend Charles Lewis Hutchins (1830-1920), American Episcopal minister.

15

**There were shepherds living out in the fields nearby,
keeping watch over their flocks at night.
An angel of the Lord appeared to them
(Luke 2:8, 9 NIV).**

Old Marley was as dead as a doornail. Mind! I don't mean to say that I know, of my own knowledge, what there is particularly dead about a doornail. I might have been inclined, myself, to regard a coffin nail as the deadest piece of ironmongery in the trade. But the wisdom of our ancestors is in the simile; and my unhallowed hands shall not disturb it, or the country's done for. You will therefore permit me to repeat, emphatically, that Marley was as dead as a doornail. Scrooge knew he was dead! Of course he did. How could it be otherwise? Scrooge and he were partners for I don't know how many years. Scrooge was his sole executor, his sole administrator, his sole assign, his sole residual legatee, his sole friend, and sole mourner. And even Scrooge was not so dreadfully cut up by the sad event, but that he was an excellent man of business on the very day of the funeral, and solemnised it with an undoubted bargain. The mention of Marley's funeral brings me back to the point I started from. There is no doubt that Marley was dead. This must be distinctly understood, or nothing wonderful can come of the story I am going to relate. If we were not perfectly convinced that Hamlet's father died before the play began, there would be nothing more remarkable in his taking a stroll at night, in an easterly wind, upon his own ramparts, than there would be in any other middle-aged gentleman rashly turning out after dark in a breezy spot – say Saint Paul's Churchyard, for instance – literally to astonish his son's weak mind. Scrooge never painted out Old Marley's name. There it stood, years afterwards, above the warehouse door: Scrooge and Marley. The firm was known as Scrooge and Marley. Sometimes people new to the business called Scrooge, and sometimes Marley, but he answered to both names. It was all the same to him. Oh! But he was a tightfisted hand at the grindstone, Scrooge! A squeezing, wrenching, grasping, scraping, clutching, covetous, old sinner! Hard and sharp as flint, from which no steel hand had ever struck out generous fire; secret, and self-contained, and solitary as an oyster. The cold within him froze his old features, nipped his pointed nose, shrivelled his cheek, stiffened his gait; made his eyes red, his thin lips blue; and spoke out shrewdly in his grating voice. A frosty rime was on his head, and on his eyebrows, and his wiry chin.[6]

Lord Jesus, I've no idea how chilly it might have been on the night your visiting angel appeared to the watching shepherds, but I shouldn't imagine it was cosy. Maybe those farm labourers, already marginalised in their lowly occupation, huddled as friends and colleagues around a crackling fire as they attended to their duties; a night-shift under the winking stars of an inky-black sky. Would they have shivered as they pulled their jackets around their tired bodies? How wonderful, then, that the initial notification of your birth came to them as a light in the darkness, in their relative isolation, as they counted the hours until they would be comfortable and safe again. Your appearance as a baby signified new life even unto the dead: all in all, in essence, a glorious summary of your incarnation.

> While shepherds watched their flocks by night,
> All seated on the ground,
> An angel of the Lord came down,
> And glory shone around.[7]

---

[6] *A Christmas Carol.*
[7] From the carol of the same name by Nahum Tate (1652-1725), Irish-born poet, hymnist and lyricist.

The true light that gives light to everyone
was coming into the world
(John 1:9 NIV)

Once upon a time, of all the good days in the year, on Christmas Eve, old Scrooge sat busy in his counting house. It was cold, bleak, biting weather: foggy withal: and he could hear the people in the court outside, go wheezing up and down, beating their hands upon their breasts, and stamping their feet upon the pavement stones to warm them. The city clocks had only just gone three, but it was quite dark already – it had not been light all day – and candles were flaring in the windows of the neighbouring offices, like ruddy smears upon the palpable brown air. The fog came pouring in at every chink and keyhole, and was so dense without, that although the court was of the narrowest, the houses opposite were mere phantoms. To see the dingy cloud come drooping down, obscuring everything, one might have thought that nature lived hard by, and was brewing on a large scale. The door of Scrooge's counting house was open that he might keep his eye upon his clerk, who in a dismal little cell beyond, a sort of tank, was copying letters. Scrooge had a very small fire, but the clerk's fire was so very much smaller that it looked like one coal. But he couldn't replenish it, for Scrooge kept the coal box in his own room; and so surely as the clerk came in with the shovel, the master predicted that it would be necessary for them to part. Wherefore the clerk put on his white comforter, and tried to warm himself at the candle; in which effort, not being a man of a strong imagination, he failed.[8]

---

[8] *A Christmas Carol.*

An uninviting scenario, Lord. There is not much here to cheer the heart. Even Scrooge's 'very small fire' fails to lift the mood, offering only the tiniest amount of heat and the dimmest glow of light. And yet, how reminiscent this is, to some degree, of the scenario that probably greeted your incarnation: an unassuming situation somewhere in the back streets of Bethlehem where 'it was quite dark already'. What a humble arrival yours really was. More than likely, Lord Jesus, you were born by candlelight, or something similar: the most glorious Light of the World entering the arena of humanity in modest circumstances, shrouded by quietness and a notable absence of publicity. This juxtaposition speaks so powerfully of the type of God you are; lowly and unassuming. This cheers the heart!

O little town of Bethlehem,
How still we see thee lie!
Above thy deep and dreamless sleep
The silent stars go by;
Yet in thy dark streets shineth
The everlasting light.
The hopes and fears of all the years
Are met in thee tonight.[9]

---

[9]   From the carol of the same name by Reverend Phillips Brooks (1835-1893), American Episcopal minister.

**To us a child is born, to us a son is given . . .
And he will be called Wonderful Counsellor.
(Isaiah 9:6 NIV)**

I have kept one secret in the course of my life. I am a bashful man. Nobody would suppose it, nobody ever does suppose it, nobody ever did suppose it, but I am naturally a bashful man. This is the secret which I have never breathed until now. I might greatly move the reader by some account of the innumerable places I have not been to, the innumerable people I have not called upon or received, the innumerable social evasions I have been guilty of, solely because I am by original constitution and character a bashful man. But I will leave the reader unmoved, and proceed with the object before me. That object is to give a plain account of my travels and discoveries in the Holly Tree Inn; in which place of good entertainment for man and beast I was once snowed up. It happened in the memorable year when I parted for ever from Angela Leath, whom I was shortly to have married, on making the discovery that she preferred my bosom friend. From our schooldays I had freely admitted Edwin, in my own mind, to be far superior to myself; and, though I was grievously wounded at heart, I felt the preference to be natural, and tried to forgive them both. It was under these circumstances that I resolved to go to America – on my way to the devil. Communicating my discovery neither to Angela nor to Edwin, but resolving to write each of them an affecting letter conveying my blessing and forgiveness, which the steam tender for shore should carry to the post when I myself should be bound for the New World, far beyond recall, - I say, locking up my grief in my own breast, and consoling myself as I could with the prospect of being generous, I quietly left all I held dear, and started on the desolate journey I have mentioned.

The dead winter-time was in full dreariness when I left my chambers for ever, at five o'clock in the morning. I had shaved by candlelight, of course, and was miserably cold, and experienced that general all-pervading sensation of getting up to be hanged which I have usually found inseparable from untimely rising under such circumstances.[10]

This season, Heavenly Father, is full of sparkling beauty. It can be, for some, though, a difficult time of poignant reflection. Often, the joyous merriment of this time of year can sit awkwardly alongside moments of silent, inner painful regret, heart-searching, and contemplation. Lord, you are the only one by whom we are truly known; you know full well when we are 'locking up my grief in my own breast'. Amidst all the colourful trappings of year's end and year's beginning, draw close to those who find it all overwhelming and distressing. Be their Wonderful Counsellor.

Hail the heav'n-born Prince of Peace!
Hail the Sun of Righteousness!
Light and life to all he brings,
Ris'n with healing in his wings.
Mild he lays his glory by,
Born that man no more may die;
Born to raise the sons of earth,
Born to give us second birth.
Hark! the herald angels sing:
'Glory to the new-born King!' [11]

[10]   *The Holly Tree* (or *The Holly Tree Inn*).
[11]   From the carol *Hark! the herald angels sing* by Charles Wesley (1707-1788), Anglican clergyman and prolific hymnwriter.

In the sixth month of Elizabeth's pregnancy, God sent the
angel Gabriel to Nazareth, a town in Galilee, to a virgin
pledged to be married to a man named Joseph,
a descendant of David. The virgin's name was Mary.
(Luke 1:26, 27 NIV)

'Don't be angry, uncle. Come! Dine with us tomorrow.' Scrooge said that he would see him – yes, indeed he did. He went the whole length of the expression, and said that he would see him in that extremity first. 'But why?' cried Scrooge's nephew. 'Why?' 'Why did you get married?' said Scrooge. 'Because I fell in love.' 'Because you fell in love!' growled Scrooge, as if that were the only one thing in the world more ridiculous than a merry Christmas. 'Good afternoon!' 'Nay, uncle, but you never came to see me before that happened. Why give it as a reason for not coming now?' 'Good afternoon,' said Scrooge. 'I want nothing from you; I ask nothing of you; why cannot we be friends?' 'Good afternoon,' said Scrooge. 'I am sorry, with all my heart, to find you so resolute. We have never had any quarrel, to which I have been a party. But I have made the trial in homage to

Christmas, and I'll keep my Christmas humour to the last. So a merry Christmas, Uncle!' 'Good afternoon,' said Scrooge. 'And a happy New Year!' 'Good afternoon,' said Scrooge. His nephew left the room without an angry word, notwithstanding. He stopped at the out door to bestow the greetings of the season on the clerk, who, cold as he was, was warmer than Scrooge; for he returned them cordially. 'There's another fellow,' muttered Scrooge; who overheard him: 'my clerk, with fifteen shillings a week, and a wife and family, talking about a merry Christmas. I'll retire to Bedlam.'[12]

Love and marriage, Lord – what a life-changing difference that package can make to individuals and families. A beautiful difference, most often, as a new member of the established family unit is welcomed and accepted. I pray for those who, like Mary and Joseph, are embarking upon the first formal steps of a relational life together, with all its experiences – and pitfalls! I pray too for those who, like Scrooge's nephew, are either newlyweds or whose experience of married life is still fresh and fledgling. Bless all such with your guidance and joy, Lord. And, should there be factions arising where love meets with hostility or resentment, and where awkward disruption has arisen on account of an engagement or a marriage, then I pray for your help, for all concerned. May this season of goodwill resonate especially within the lives of those included in these prayers.

Joseph was an old man,
An old man was he,
He married Virgin Mary,
The Queen of Galilee.[13]

---

[12]   *A Christmas Carol.*
[13]   From *The cherry tree carol*, an ancient ballad, reportedly sung in some form at the Feast of Corpus Christi in the early fifteenth century.

Joseph also went up from the town of Nazareth in Galilee to Judea, to Bethlehem the town of David, because he belonged to the house and line of David.
(Luke 2:4 NIV)

High up in the steeple of an old church, far above the light and murmur of the town and far below the flying clouds that shadow it, is the wild and dreary place at night: and high up in the steeple of an old church, dwelt the chimes I tell of. They were old chimes, trust me. Centuries ago, these bells had been baptized by bishops: so many centuries ago, that the register of their baptism was lost long, long before the memory of man, and no one knew their names. They had had their Godfathers and Godmothers, these bells (for my own part, by the way, I would rather incur the responsibility of being Godfather to a bell than a boy), and had their silver mugs no doubt, besides. But time had mowed down their sponsors, and Henry the Eighth had melted down their mugs; and they now hung, nameless and mugless, in the church tower. Not speechless, though. Far from it. They had clear, loud, lusty, sounding voices, had these bells; and far and wide they might be heard upon the wind. Much too sturdy chimes were they, to be dependent on the pleasure of the wind, moreover; for, fighting gallantly against it when it took an adverse whim, they would pour their cheerful notes into a listening ear right royally; and bent on being heard, on stormy night, by some poor mother watching a sick child, or some lone wife whose husband was at sea, they had been sometimes known to bear a blustering nor 'wester; aye.[14] [15]

---

[14] *The Chimes.*
[15] Within Roman Catholicism, it is common to 'baptise' bells when they are installed, giving them names (usually saints' names), and assigning them godparents. When the large bell in Notre-Dame Cathedral, Emmanuel, was installed, in 1681, it was named in honour of a chaplain who financed the project.

*Lord Jesus, what a distinctly human lineage was yours! A
king or two, rulers of lands, a prostitute, a land owner, and
a handful of patriarchs, to name just a few. You came to us,
in your incarnation, born of the Virgin Mary and adopted
by the carpenter Joseph, as one truly and properly God and
truly and properly man. Quite possibly, some of the details of
your biological ancestry have been 'lost long, long before the
memory of man', in terms of specific information, yet the fact
remains that you subjected yourself to the terms and conditions
of inheriting a human bloodline. This is remarkable; that you,
as God, should condescend in such a way, to reach fallen
humanity: God made flesh.*

God of God, Light of Light,
Lo! He abhors not the Virgin's womb;
Very God, begotten not created.

O come, let us adore him,
O come, let us adore him,
O come, let us adore him,
Christ the Lord.[16]

---

[16]   From the carol *O come, all ye faithful*, attributed to various people.

God so loved the world that he gave his one and only Son.
(John 3:16 NIV)

They were portly gentlemen, pleasant to behold, and now stood, with their hats off, in Scrooge's office. They had books and papers in their hands, and bowed to him. 'Scrooge and Marley's, I believe,' said one of the gentlemen, referring to his list. 'Have I the pleasure of addressing Mr. Scrooge, or Mr. Marley?' 'Mr. Marley has been dead these seven years,' Scrooge replied. 'He died seven years ago, this very might.' 'We have no doubt his liberality is well represented by his surviving partner,' said the gentleman, presenting his credentials. It certainly was; for they had been two kindred spirits. At the ominous word 'liberality,' Scrooge frowned, and shook his head, and handed the credentials back. 'At this festive season of the year, Mr. Scrooge,' said the gentlemen, taking up a pen, 'it is more than usually desirable that we should make some slight provision for the poor and destitute, who suffer greatly at the present time. Many thousands are in want of common necessaries; hundreds of thousands are in want of common comforts, Sir.' 'Are there no prisons?' asked Scrooge. 'Plenty of prisons,' said the gentleman, laying down the pen again. 'And the union workhouses?' demanded Scrooge. 'Are they still in operation?' 'They are. Still,' returned the gentleman, 'I wish I could say they were not.' 'The treadmill and the Poor Law are in full vigour, then?' said Scrooge. 'Both very busy, Sir.' 'Oh! I was afraid, from what you said at first, that something had occurred to stop them in their useful course,' said Scrooge. 'I am very glad to hear it.' 'Under the impression that they scarcely furnish Christian cheer of mind or body to the multitude,' returned the gentleman, 'a few of us are endeavouring to raise a fund to buy the poor some meat and drink, and a means of warmth. We choose this time, because it is a time, of all others, when want is keenly felt, and abundance rejoices. What shall I put you down for?' 'Nothing!' Scrooge replied. 'You wish to be anonymous?' 'I wish to be left alone,' said Scrooge. 'Since you ask me what I wish, gentlemen, that is my answer. I don't make merry myself at Christmas and I can't afford to make idle merry. I help to support the establishments I have mentioned – they cost enough; and those who are badly off must go there.'[17]

Father God, you gave your only begotten Son, the babe of Bethlehem, simply because, as the adage reminds us, it is possible to give without loving, but impossible to love without giving. You gave of yourself; the triune Godhead reaching out to a world whose want of a Saviour was 'keenly felt'. Thank you, Lord Jesus, for coming to find 'those who are badly off' in spiritual terms. Wonderful love, given to us from heaven above.

God give ye merry Christmas tide,
And give ye all to see
How blessed 'tis to give and know
The grace of charity;
Rejoice! for once at Bethlehem,
To give his life away,
Our blessed Master Jesus Christ,
Was born on Christmas Day.[18]

---

17 *A Christmas Carol.*
18 From a traditional old English carol. Authorship uncertain.

**Herds of camels will cover your land, young camels of
Midian and Ephah. And all from Sheba will come, bearing
gold and incense and proclaiming the praise of the Lord.
(Isaiah 60:6 NIV)**

I have been looking on, this evening, at a merry company of children assembled round that pretty German toy, a Christmas tree. The tree was planted in the middle of a great round table, and towered high above their heads. It was brilliantly lighted by a multitude of little tapers; and everywhere sparkled and glittered with bright objects. There were rosy-cheeked dolls, hiding behind the green leaves; and there were real watches (with movable hands, at least, and an endless capacity of being wound up) dangling from innumerable twigs; there were French-polished tables, chairs, bedsteads, wardrobes, eight-day clocks, and various other articles of domestic furniture (wonderfully made, in tin, at Wolverhampton), perched among the boughs, as if in preparation for some fairy housekeeping; there were jolly, broad-faced little men, much more agreeable in appearance than many real men – and no wonder, for their heads took off, and showed them to be full of sugar-plums; there were fiddles and drums; there were tambourines, books, work-boxes, paint-boxes, sweetmeat-boxes, peep-show boxes, and all kinds of boxes; there were trinkets for the elder girls, far brighter than any grown-up gold and jewels; there were baskets and pincushions in all devices; there were guns, swords, and banners; there were witches standing in enchanted rings of pasteboard, to tell fortunes; there were teetotums, humming tops, needle-cases, pen-wipers, smelling-bottles, conversation-cards, bouquet-holders; real fruit, made artificially dazzling with gold leaf; imitation apples, pears, and walnuts, crammed with surprises; in short, as a pretty child, before, me, delightedly whispered to another pretty child, her bosom friend, 'There was everything, and more.'[19]

<hr>

What a marvellous scene, Lord: a celebration of your birth, a party, a family gathering, a rekindling of friendships, and a time of celebration. These words paint a thousand pictures! Carry my imagination away, Lord, to the scene of which Isaiah the prophet spoke; those of Sheba trekking in pilgrimage and homage, bearing 'grown-up gold' and very possibly 'trinkets' and 'jewels' too, heralding the arrival of deity nigh. This Christmas, Lord, grant me a quiet corner of prayerful reflection, so that I too may worship and give honour due.

<hr>

Frankincense to offer have I;
Incense owns a deity nigh;
Prayer and praising, voices raising,
Worshipping God on high.[20]

[19]   *A Christmas Tree.*
[20]   From the carol *We three kings of orient are* by John Henry Hopkins, Jr. (1820-1891), American ecclesiologist.

**When the set time had fully come,
God sent his Son, born of a woman.
(Galatians 4:4 NIV)**

Time was, with most of us, when Christmas Day encircling all our limited world like a magic ring, left nothing out for us to miss or seek; bound together all our home enjoyments, affections, and hopes; grouped everything and everyone around the Christmas fire; and made the little picture shining in our bright young eyes, complete. Time came, and perhaps all so soon, when our thoughts overleaped that narrow boundary; when there was someone (very dear, we thought then, very beautiful, and absolutely perfect) wanting to the fulness of our happiness; when we were wanting too (or we thought so, which was just as well) at the Christmas hearth by which that someone sat; and when we intertwined with every wreath and garland of our life that someone's name. That was the time for the bright visionary Christmases which have long arisen from us to show faintly, after summer rain, in the palest edges of the rainbow! That was the time for the beatified enjoyment of the things that were to be, and never were, and yet the things that were so real in our resolute hope that it would be hard to say, now, what realities achieved since, have been stronger![21]

How quickly, Lord, relatively speaking, time passes. Time rolls its sons and daughters along, regardless of status, wealth, or privilege. One minute, so it seems, we are children, thrilled with all the fripperies of Christmas Day and bursting with excitement. And, then, almost before we know it, we look around and notice that we

[21]   *What Christmas is as we grow older.*

are no longer as young as we once were, when even Christmas is a different experience. It has to be like that, of course, as we mature and develop. Your timing, Lord, is always perfect, down to the heartbeat; you are never too early, and you are never late. Teach me the art of entrusting each of my passing days into your hands, knowing for sure that there won't be any mistakes made on your part.

For lo! the days are hastening on,
By prophet bards foretold,
When, with the ever-circling years,
Shall come the age of gold;
When peace shall over all the earth
Her ancient splendours fling,
And the whole world sends back the song
Which now the angels sing.[22]

[22] From the carol *It came upon the midnight clear* by Edmund Hamilton Sears (1810-1876), American Unitarian minister and author.

There was a man in Jerusalem called Simeon . . . It had been revealed to him by the Holy Spirit that he would not die before he had seen the Lord's Messiah.
(Luke 2:25, 26 NIV)

Wet weather was the worst; the cold, damp, clammy wet, that wrapped [Toby Veck] up like a moist great-coat – the only kind of great-coat Toby owned, or could have added to his comfort by dispensing with. Wet days, when the rain came slowly, thickly, obstinately down; when the street's throat, like his own, was choked with mist; when smoking umbrellas passed and re-passed, spinning round and round like so many teetotums, as they knocked against each other on the crowded footway, throwing off a little whirlpool of uncomfortable sprinklings; when gutters brawled and waterspouts were full and noisy; when the wet from the projecting stones and ledges of the church fell drip, drip, drip on Toby, making the wisp of straw on which he stood mere mud in no time; those were the days that tried him. Then, indeed, you might see Toby looking anxiously out from his shelter in an angle of the church wall – such a meagre shelter that in summer time it never cast a shadow thicker than a good-sized, walking stick upon the sunny pavement – with a disconsolate and lengthened face. But coming out, a minute afterwards, to warm himself by exercise, and trotting up and down some dozen times, he would brighten even then, and go back more brightly to his niche. They called him Trotty from his pace, which meant speed if it didn't make it. He could have walked faster perhaps; most likely; but rob him of his trot, and Toby would have taken to his bed and died. It bespattered him with mud in dirty weather; it cost him a world of trouble; he could have walked with infinitely greater ease; but that was one reason for his clinging to it so tenaciously. A weak, small, spare old man, he was a very Hercules, this Toby, in his good intentions. He loved to earn his money. He was delighted to believe – Toby was very poor, and couldn't well afford to part with a delight – that he was worth his salt . . . Thus, even when he came out of his nook to warm himself on a wet day, Toby trotted. Making, with his leaky shoes, a crooked line of slushy footprints in the mire; and blowing on his chilly hands and rubbing them against each other, poorly defended from the searching cold by threadbare mufflers of grey worsted, with a private apartment only for the thumb, and a common room or tap for the rest of the fingers; Toby, with his knees bent and his cane beneath his arm, still trotted. Falling out into the road to look up at the belfry when the chimes resounded, Toby trotted still. [23]

'Looking anxiously out from his shelter in an angle of the church wall.' 'A weak, small, spare old man.' Was that Simeon, Lord? Waiting and watching, and one whose devout attention is recorded in Scripture. Gracious Lord, you do not overlook our devotion. Make me a Simeon; focussed on matters of salvation.

The King of all kings to this world being brought,
Small store of fine linen to wrap him was sought;
But when she had swaddled her young Son so sweet,
Within an ox manger she laid him to sleep.
To teach us humility all this was done,
And learn we from thence haughty pride for to shun:
A manger his cradle who came from above,
The great God of mercy, of peace, and of love.[24]

[23]   *The Chimes.*
[24]   From the c.1661 carol and English folk song *A virgin unspotted*. Authorship uncertain.

**He came to that which was his own,
but his own did not receive him.
(John 1:11 NIV)**

I . . . come home at Christmas. We all do, or we all should. We all come home, or ought to come home, for a short holiday – the longer, the better – from the great boarding-school, where we are forever working at our arithmetical slates, to take, and give a rest. As to going a-visiting, where can we not go . . . On, by low-lying, misty grounds, through fens and fogs, up long hills, winding dark as caverns between thick plantations, almost shutting out the sparkling stars; so, out on broad heights, until we stop at last, with sudden silence, at an avenue. The gate-bell has a deep, half-awful sound in the frosty air; the gate swings open on its hinges; and, as we drive up to a great house, the glancing lights grow larger in the windows, and the opposing rows of trees seem to fall solemnly back on either side, to give us place. At intervals, all day, a frightened hare has shot across this whitened turf; or the distant clatter of a herd of deer trampling the hard frost, has, for the minute, crushed the silence too. Their watchful eyes beneath the fern may be shining now, if we could see them, like the icy dewdrops on the leaves; but they are still, and all is still. And so, the lights growing larger, and the trees falling back before us, and closing up again behind, as if to forbid retreat, we come to the house. There is probably a smell of roasted chestnuts and other good comfortable things all the time, for we are telling winter stories – ghost stories – or more shame for us – round the Christmas fire; and we have never stirred, except to draw a little nearer to it.[25]

---

[25]   *A Christmas Tree.*

Lord Jesus, you are, ultimately, our great 'home'. Our souls are at rest in you; within your love, surrounded by your presence. That is where – and how – we live our best lives, in terms of our holistic natures. Yet, we do not always want to come home. We are complex beings, and oftentimes we prefer to go our own way; to leave home, so to speak. You came for us – Christmas tells us so – yet sometimes we choose not to come to you. Forgive us such ungrateful wanderings, Lord, and in your gracious love, reconcile us to yourself, the focus of our eternal wellbeing. 'We all come home, or ought to come home': let it be.

Hark! the herald angels sing
'Glory to the new-born king
Peace on earth and mercy mild
God and sinners reconciled.'
Joyful all ye nations rise,
Join the triumph of the skies;
With the angelic host proclaim:
'Christ is born in Bethlehem.'
Hark! the herald angels sing:
'Glory to the new-born king' [26]

---

[26]   From *Hark! the herald angels sing.*

35

Your God will come . . . he will come to save you.
Then will the eyes of the blind be opened.
(Isaiah 35:4, 5 NIV)

At length the hour of shutting up the counting-house arrived. With an ill-will Scrooge dismounted from his stool, and tacitly admitted the fact to the expectant clerk . . . who instantly snuffed his candle out, and put on his hat. 'You'll want all day tomorrow, I suppose?' said Scrooge. 'If quite convenient, sir.' 'It's not convenient,' said Scrooge, 'and it's not fair. If I was to stop you half-a-crown for it, you'd think yourself ill-used, I'll be bound?' The clerk smiled faintly. 'And yet,' said Scrooge, 'you don't think *me* ill-used, when I pay a day's wages for no work.' The clerk observed that it was only once a year. 'A poor excuse for picking a man's pocket every twenty-fifth of December!' said Scrooge, buttoning his great-coat to the chin. 'But I suppose you must have the whole day. Be here all the earlier next morning.' The clerk promised that he would; and Scrooge walked out with a growl. The office was closed in a twinkling, and the clerk, with the long ends of his white comforter dangling below his waist (for he boasted no great-coat), went down a slide on Cornhill, at the end of a lane of boys, twenty times, in honour of its being Christmas Eve, and then ran home to Camden Town as hard as he could pelt, to play at blind man's bluff. Scrooge took his melancholy dinner in his usual melancholy tavern; and having read all the newspapers, and beguiled the rest of the evening with his banker's book, went home to bed. He lived in chambers which had once belonged to his deceased partner. They were a gloomy suite of rooms, in a lowering pile of building up a yard, where it had so little business to be, that one could scarcely help fancying it must have been there when it was a young house, playing at hide-and-seek with other houses, and forgotten the way out again. It was old enough now, and dreary enough, for nobody lived in it but Scrooge, the other rooms being all let out as offices. The yard was so dark that even Scrooge, who knew its every stone, was fain to grope with his hands. The fog and frost so hung about the black old gateway of the house, that it seemed as if the Genius of the Weather[27] sat in mournful meditation on the threshold.[28]

Lord Jesus, your incarnation gloriously fulfilled the prophecy of Isaiah 35. You came to us, as God made flesh. We need not, therefore, like Scrooge, grope about in darkness. You came to us, to cure our spiritual blindness so that we may see love and truth. I pray for those whose lives are eked out in melancholic gloom, spiritually-speaking. Come to them with light and revelation, that the true message of Christmas may arise in their hearts.

A light came out of darkness;
No light, no hope, had we,
Till Jesus came from heaven
Our light and hope to be.[29]

[27] As in genie.
[28] *A Christmas Carol.*
[29] From the carol of the same name by William Hawley (c.1870-1929), Canadian musician with the First Baptist Church and The Salvation Army.

**You know the grace of our Lord Jesus Christ, that though
he was rich, yet for your sake he became poor, so that you
through his poverty might become rich.
(2 Corinthians 8:9 NIV)**

Ah! The doll's house! – of which I was not the proprietor,
but where I visited. I don't admire the Houses of Parliament
half so much as that stone-fronted mansion with real glass
windows, and doorsteps, and a real balcony – greener than I ever
see now, except at watering places; and even they afford but a
poor imitation. And though it *did* open all at once, the entire
house-front (which was a blow, I admit, as cancelling the fiction
of a staircase), it was but to shut it up again, and I could believe.
Even open, there were three distinct rooms in it: a sitting-room
and bedroom, elegantly furnished, and best of all, a kitchen, with
uncommonly soft fire-irons, a plentiful assortment of diminutive
utensils – oh, the warm frying pan! – and a tin man-cook in
profile, who was always going to fry two fish. What Barmecide[30]
justice have I done to the noble feasts wherein the set of wooden
platters figured, each with its own peculiar delicacy, as a ham or
turkey, glued tight to it, and garnished with something green,
which I recollect as moss! Could all the temperance societies of
those later days, united, give me such a tea-drinking as I have had
through the means of yonder little set of blue crockery, which
really would hold liquid (it ran out of the small wooden cask, I
recollect, and tasted of matches), and which made tea, nectar.
And if the two legs of the ineffectual little sugar tongs did tumble
over one another, and want purpose, like Punch's, what does it
matter! And if I did once shriek out, as a poisoned child, and

[30] Illusory and therefore disappointing.

strike the fashionable company with consternation, by reason of having drunk a little teaspoon, inadvertently dissolved in hot tea, I was never the worse for it, except by a powder![31]

Ornaments hanging from, or surrounding, a Christmas tree, Lord Jesus: did you ever play with toys? Did your childhood include fascinating things for you to play with? Were any of the kinds of amusements described here, yours too, as a little boy, growing up? Or were your early years a much more serious affair altogether? Did a sense of destiny hang over your boyhood? I like to think you played, and that your incarnation included fun and laughter. Lord, I pray for children all around the world for whom Christmas is a sad time, a lonely time, perhaps; boys and girls whose parents can't provide anything much for them, and for whom a Christmas present such as a doll's house is but a fanciful dream. Help them, I pray, especially when divisions between rich and poor are highlighted.

He came down to earth from heaven,
Who is God and Lord of all,
And his shelter was a stable,
And his cradle was a stall;
With the poor, and mean, and lowly,
Lived on earth our Saviour holy.[32]

---

[31]   *A Christmas Tree.*
[32]   From the carol *Once in royal David's city* by Cecil Frances Alexander (1818-1895), Anglo-Irish hymn writer and poet.

Jesus grew in wisdom and stature.
(Luke 2:52 NIV)

As we grow older, let us be more thankful that the circle of our Christmas associations and of the lessons that they bring, expands! Let us welcome every one of them, and summon them to take their places by the Christmas hearth. Welcome, old aspirations, glittering creatures of an ardent fancy, to your shelter underneath the holly! We know you, and have not outlived you yet. Welcome, old projects and old loves, however fleeting, to your nooks among the steadier lights that burn around us. Welcome, all that was ever real to our hearts; and for the earnestness that made you real, thanks to heaven! Do we build no Christmas candles in the clouds now? Let our thoughts, fluttering like butterflies among these flowers of children, bear witness! Before this boy, there stretches out a future, brighter than we ever looked on in our old romantic time, but bright with honour and with truth. Around this little head on which the sunny curls lie heaped, the graces sport, as prettily, as airily, as when there was no scythe within the reach of Time to shear away the curls of our first-love. Upon another girl's face near it – placider but smiling bright – a quiet and contented little face, we see Home fairly written. Shining from the word, as rays shine from a star, we see how, when our graves are old, other hopes than ours are young, other hearts than ours are moved; how other ways are smoothed; how other happiness blooms, repines, and decays – no, not decays, for other homes and other bands of children, not yet in being nor for ages yet to be, arise, and bloom and ripen to the end of all. Welcome, everything! Welcome, alike what has been, and what never was, and what we hope may be, to your shelter underneath the holly, to your places round the Christmas fire, where what is sits open-hearted! In

40

yonder shadow, do we see obtruding furtively upon the blaze, an enemy's face? By Christmas Day do we forgive him! If the injury he has done us may admit of such companionship, let him come here and take his place. If otherwise, unhappily, let him go hence, assured that we will never injure nor accuse him.[33]

A season of great rejoicing, Lord, and of laughter, fun and relaxation. Also, a season for reflection and contemplation: a season for forgiveness, even, and making amends; letting bygones be just that, so far as it rests with us to do so. A season for letting go, and for quietly, privately, coming to terms with the vagaries of life and humanity. Lord Jesus, as you grew from being the manger-baby to the holy toddler, towards childhood, adolescence, and adulthood, you fully shared our common lot: you shied away from nothing. The sharpest stones that prick our feet, you felt too. You matured physically – God made flesh, Immanuel – and in doing so, entered this life, truly as one of us.

For he is our childhood's pattern;
Day by day, like us he grew;
He was little, weak and helpless,
Tears and smiles like us he knew;
And he feeleth for our sadness,
And he shareth in our gladness.[34]

---

[33] *What Christmas is as we grow older.*
[34] From *Once in royal David's city.*

41

**'You will conceive and give birth to a son, and you are
to call him Jesus' . . . 'How will this be,'
Mary asked the angel, 'since I am a virgin?'
(Luke 1:31-34 NIV)**

S crooge had as little of what is called fancy about him as any man in the city of London, even including – which is a bold word – the corporation, aldermen, and livery. Let it also be borne in mind that Scrooge had not bestowed one thought on Marley, since his last mention of his seven-years' dead partner . . . And then let any man explain to me, if he can, how it happened that Scrooge, having his key in the lock of the door, saw in the knocker, without its undergoing any intermediate process of change – not a knocker, but Marley's face. Marley's face. It was not in impenetrable shadow as other objects in the yard were, but had a dismal light about it, like a bad lobster in a dark cellar. It was not angry or ferocious, but it looked at Scrooge as Marley used to look: with ghostly spectacles turned up on its ghostly forehead. The hair was curiously stirred, as if by breath or hot air; and, though the eyes were wide open, they were perfectly motionless. That, and its livid colour, made it horrible; but its horror seemed to be in spite of the face and beyond its control, rather than a part of its own expression. As Scrooge looked fixedly at this phenomenon, it was a knocker again. To say that he was not startled, or that his blood was not conscious of a terrible sensation to which it had been a stranger from infancy, would be untrue. But he put his hand upon the key he had relinquished, turned it sturdily, walked in, and lighted his candle. He did pause, with a moment's irresolution, before he shut the door; and he did look cautiously behind it first, as if he half expected to be terrified with the sight of Marley's pigtail sticking out into the hall. But there was nothing on the back of the door, except the screws and nuts that held the knocker on, so he said 'Pooh, pooh!' and closed it with a bang. The sound resounded through the house like thunder. Every room above, and every cask in the wine-merchant's cellars below, appeared to have a separate peal of echoes of its own. Scrooge was not a man to be frightened by echoes. He fastened the door, and walked across the hall, and up the stairs; slowly too: trimming his candle as he went.[35]

This is something and nothing, Lord: a brilliantly-written tale of an elderly miser and a make-believe apparition. Fascinating reading and a story superbly articulated, but that's all, in terms of reality. Yet, how slow we are at times, Lord, to accept accounts of supernatural events referred to in the Bible; slower still to register their significance. Not faces appearing in door-knockers as if by magic, but matters that carry spiritual importance. Your birth, for example; born as the biological son of a virgin! How can this be, except as a sovereign miracle? This seems incredible, yet it holds fast as one of the basic and best tenets of Christian belief. Lord Jesus: miraculously begotten.

Ave! Ave Maria!
To gladden priest and people the angelus shall ring from every steeple, to sound his virgin birth.
Alleluia!
Ave! Ave Maria! Ave! Ave Maria! [36]

---

[35]   *A Christmas Carol.*
[36]   From the carol *Hail! Blessed Virgin Mary!* by George Ratcliffe Woodward (1848-1934), Anglican priest.

**What is mankind that you are mindful of them,
human beings that you care for them?
(Psalm 8:4 NIV)**

Toby . . . continued to trot backwards and forwards: musing as he went, and talking to himself. 'It seems as if we can't go right, or do right, or be righted,' said Toby. 'I hadn't much schooling, myself, when I was young; and I can't make out whether we have any business on the face of the earth, or not. Sometimes I think we must have – a little; and sometimes I think we must be intruding. I get so puzzled sometimes that I am not even able to make up my mind whether there is any good at all in us, or whether we are born bad. We seem to be dreadful things; we seem to give a deal of trouble; we are always being complained of and guarded against. One way or other, we fill the papers. Talk of a New Year!' said Toby, mournfully. 'I can bear up as well as another man at most times; better than a good many, for I am as strong as a lion, and all men ain't; but supposing it should really be that we have no right to a New Year – supposing we really *are* intruding.'[37]

Lord, we can all identify with Toby, to one degree or another: 'imposter syndrome' has the potential to make any of us wonder why we are here, why we were born, and even to doubt the worth and validity of our very existence. We too, if we are honest, 'trot backwards and forwards' at times, Toby-like, wondering if we might somehow be intruding. Yet, your incarnation demonstrates the immense worth placed upon a human soul in

[37]   *The Chimes.*

the courts of heaven; that you should visit us to reassure us of just how precious we are in your sight. Thank you for coming, and in doing so, quite emphatically refuting imposter syndrome. Thank you for this divine vote of confidence.

God rest ye merry, gentlemen,
Let nothing you dismay;
Remember Christ, our Saviour,
Was born on Christmas Day
To save us all from Satan's pow'r
When we had gone astray.

O tidings of comfort and joy,
Comfort and joy,
O tidings of comfort and joy [38]

[38] Author unknown. (This carol is the only one mentioned in Dickens' *A Christmas Carol.*)

**In the past God spoke to our ancestors through
the prophets at many times and in various ways,
but in these last days he has spoken to us by his Son.
(Hebrews 1:1 NIV)**

Toby, putting a hand on each knee, bent down his nose to the basket, and took a long inspiration at the lid; the grin upon his withered face expanding in the process, as if he were inhaling laughing gas. 'Ah! It's very nice,' said Toby. 'It ain't – I suppose it ain't polonies?' 'No, no, no!' cried Meg, delighted. 'Nothing like polonies!' 'No,' said Toby, after another sniff. 'It's – it's a mellower than polonies. It's very nice. It improves every moment. It's too decided for trotters. Ain't it?' Meg was in an ecstasy. He could not have gone wider of the mark that trotters – except polonies. 'Liver?' said Toby, communing with himself. 'No. There's a mildness about it that don't answer to liver. Pettitoes? No. It ain't faint enough to pettitoes. It wants the stringiness of cocks' heads. And I know it ain't sausages. I'll tell you what it is. It's chitterlings!' 'No, it ain't!' cried Meg, in a burst of delight. 'No, it ain't!' 'Why, what am I a-thinking of!' said Toby, suddenly recovering a position as near the perpendicular as it was possible for him to assume. 'I shall forget my own name next. It's tripe!' Tripe it was; and Meg, in high joy, protested he should say, in half a minute more, it was the best tripe ever stewed.[39]

What a lot of guesswork, Lord! Jumping from one incorrect conclusion to another, with several stabs at guessing the right

[39] *The Chimes.*

answer, covering all sorts of options. How thankful we should be, Heavenly Father, that the life of Jesus has removed the need for any similar speculation and conjecture regarding your being and nature. We are not left to guess what you might be like, working our way through some kind of list and making stabs in the dark. We are not abandoned to supposing or assuming: rather, we see it all in Jesus. Thank you, Lord, for this revelation: in the babe of Bethlehem, we see the face of God. In Christ, we know God with us. Your identity has been revealed, and confirmed, in Scripture. The mystery is solved! The Prince has come amongst us.

This stable is a Prince's court,
The crib his chair of state,
The beasts are parcel on his pomp,[40]
The wooden dish his plate;
The persons in that poor attire
His royal liveries wear;
The Prince himself is come from heaven,
This pomp is prizèd there. [41]

[40] Possibly, something like, from old English: 'a pack of animals surrounds his majesty' – a description of the fact that, in Christ, God appeared amongst the lowly beasts of earth.

[41] From the carol *Behold a silly tender babe* by Robert Southwell (1561-1595), English Jesuit poet and martyr. (The word 'silly,' in Southwell's day, meant artless, or without guile.)

**Make pomegranates of blue, purple and scarlet yarn around
the hem of the robe, with gold bells between them. The gold
bells and the pomegranates are to alternate around the hem
of the robe. Aaron must wear it when he ministers.
The sound of the bells will be heard when he enters the Holy
Place before the LORD and when he comes out.
(Exodus 28:33-35 NIV)**

[Scrooge] took off his cravat; put on his dressing-gown and slippers, and his nightcap; and sat down before the fire to take his gruel. It was a very low fire indeed; nothing on such a bitter night. He was obliged to sit close to it, and brood over it, before he could extract the least sensation of warmth from such a handful of fuel. The fireplace was an old one, built by some Dutch merchant long ago, and paved all round with quaint Dutch tiles, designed to illustrate the Scriptures. There were Cains and Abels, Pharaohs' daughters, Queens of Sheba, Angelic messengers descending through the air on clouds like feather-beds, Abrahams, Belshazzars, apostles putting off to sea in butter-boats, hundreds of figures to attract his thoughts; and yet that face of Marley, seven years dead, came like the ancient prophet's rod, and swallowed up the whole. If each smooth tile had been a blank at first, with power to shape some picture on its surface from the disjointed fragments of his thoughts, there would have been a copy of Marley's head on every one. 'Humbug!' said Scrooge; and walked across the room. After several turns, he sat down again. As he threw his head back in the chair, his glance happened to rest upon a bell, a disused bell, that hung in the room, and communicated for some purpose now forgotten with a chamber in the highest storey of the building. It was with great astonishment, and with a strange, inexplicable dread, that as he looked, he saw this bell begin to swing. It swung so softly in the in the outset that it scarcely made a sound; but soon it rang out loudly, and so did every bell in the house.[42]

Lord Jesus, bells ring out all around the world when Christmas is celebrated; each peal signifying joy and delight. Our great High Priest has come, to minister redemption for the lands where sweet chiming bells echo the theme. Aaron appeared as a prototype, Lord; a foreshadowing of the ultimate priestly sacrifice. We rejoice that 'the sound of the bells will be heard', nowadays, in jubilation. Their clanging reminds us of your visitation, Lord Jesus; that you entered this world on behalf of those in darkness; us, whose lives were bleak and cold, in sin, with only 'the least sensation of warmth', spiritually speaking. Our dread has gone, because of you.

I heard the bells on Christmas Day
Their old familiar carols play,
And wild and sweet the words repeat
Of peace on earth, goodwill to men.

I thought how, as the day had come,
The belfries of all Christendom
Had rolled along th'unbroken song
Of peace on earth, goodwill to men.[43]

---

[42]   *A Christmas Carol.*
[43]   From the carol of the same title by Henry Wadsworth Longfellow (1807-1882), American poet, educator, and professor of literature.

For to us a child is born, to us a son is given . . .
Wonderful Counsellor . . . Prince of Peace.
(Isaiah 9:6, 7 NIV)

Scrooge awoke, it was so dark, that looking out of bed, he could scarcely distinguish the transparent window from the opaque walls of his chamber. He was endeavouring to pierce the darkness with his ferret eyes, when the chimes of a neighbouring church struck the four quarters. So he listened for the hour. To his great astonishment the heavy bell went on from six to seven and from seven to eight, and regularly up to twelve; then stopped. Twelve! It was past two when he went to bed. The clock was wrong. An icicle must have got into the works. Twelve! He touched the spring of his repeater, to correct the most preposterous clock. Its rapid little pulse beat twelve; and stopped. 'Why, it isn't possible,' said Scrooge, 'that I can have slept through a whole day and far into another night. It isn't possible that anything has happened to the sun, and this is twelve at noon!' The idea being an alarming one, he scrambled out of bed, and groped his way to the window. He was obliged to rub the frost off with the sleeve of his dressing gown before he could see anything; and could see very little then. All he could make out was, that it was still very foggy and extremely cold, and that there was no noise of people running to and fro, and making a great stir, as there unquestionably would have been if night had beaten off bright day, and taken possession of the world. This was a great relief . . . Scrooge went to bed again, and thought, and thought, and thought it over and over and over, and could make nothing of it. The more he thought, the more perplexed he was; and the more he endeavoured not to think, the more he thought. Marley's ghost bothered him exceedingly.[44]

[44]   *A Christmas Carol.*

Heavenly Father, your love for us includes your concern for our mental health. Yet, I wonder if we realise that as perhaps we should? We are 'fearfully and wonderfully made' with a marvellously complex nervous system that enables us to function, know, and feel. Our brains are intricate beyond words, and marvels of neuroscience in their elaborate construction. Yet, when something within that system malfunctions, or becomes damaged, and we find ourselves alarmed, scrambling for reason, groping our way through periods of frightening perplexity, thinking, and thinking, and thinking, over and over and over, then we need your peace. Lord, in your mercy, hear our prayers today for those whose mental health is chaotic, and for whom this time of year is anything but enjoyable. Come, Lord, in all your gentle power, and still storms. Grant your counsel; your calming touch.

O come, O Bright and Morning Star,
And bring us comfort from afar!
Dispel the shadows of the night,
And turn our darkness into light.[45]

---

[45]   From *O come, o come, Emmanuel, and ransom captive Israel* and translated into English by John Mason Neale, Anglican priest and hymn writer (1818-1866).

**Mary treasured up all these things and
pondered them in her heart.
(Luke 2:19 NIV)**

Day of the month and year, November the thirtieth, one thousand eight hundred and thirty-five. London Time by the great clock of Saint Paul's, ten at night. All the lesser London churches strain their metallic throats. Some, flippantly begin before the heavy bell of the great cathedral; some, tardily begin three, four, half a dozen strokes behind it; all are in sufficiently near accord, to leave a resonance in the air, as if the winged father who devours his children, had made a sounding sweep with his gigantic scythe in flying over the city. What is this clock lower than most of the rest, and nearer to the ear, that lags so far behind tonight as to strike into the vibration alone? This is the clock of the Hospital for Foundling Children. Time was, when the foundlings were received without question in a cradle at the gate. Time is, when inquiries are made respecting them, and they are taken as by favour from the mothers who relinquish all-natural knowledge of them and claim to them for evermore. The moon is at the full, and the night is fair with light clouds. The day has been otherwise than fair, for slush and mud, thickened with the droppings of heavy fog, lie black in the streets. The veiled lady who flutters up and down near the postern-gate of the Hospital for Foundling Children has need to be well shod tonight. She flutters to and fro, avoiding the stand of the hackney-coaches, and often pausing in the shadow of the western end of the great quadrangle wall, with her face turned towards the gate. As above her there is the purity of the moonlit sky, and below her there are the defilements of the pavement, so may she, haply, be divided in her mind between two vistas of reflection or experience. As her footprints crossing and recrossing one another have made a labyrinth in the mire, so may her track in life have involved itself in an intricate and unravellable tangle.[46]

Lord Jesus, son of Mary, as this year ends and another begins, when deep and hidden memories are stirred, with much to ponder, my prayers embrace those whose lives are touched by adoption and fostering; children and parents alike. I thank you for those whose vocation is to foster or adopt, for the love they show to those entrusted into their care. Theirs is a special way of living, and a huge influence for good. I pray your blessing upon them. I pray, too, for those whose experience of fostering and adoption is laced with heartache; their lives weighed down by intricate and seemingly unravellable tangles. Whatever the circumstances, draw close to them, I ask, and impart peace. Bring healing, Lord, to children, to teenagers, to adults; to all concerned.

He neither shall be born
In house nor in hall,
Nor in the place of Paradise,
But in an ox-stall.

Mary took her baby,
She dressed him so sweet,
She laid him in a manger
All there for to sleep.[47]

---

[46]   *No Thoroughfare.* This story, written as a play, was a collaboration, authored conjointly by Dickens and his great friend, the author Wilkie Collins. This portion here was written exclusively by Charles Dickens.
[47]   From *The cherry tree carol.*

**Joseph also went up from the town of Nazareth in
Galilee to Judea, to Bethlehem the town of David . . .
He went there to register with Mary.
(Luke 2:4,5 NIV)**

How well I remember the forlorn aspect of Fleet Street when I came out of the Temple! The streetlamps flickering in the gusty north-east wind, as if the very gas were contorted with cold; the white-topped houses; the bleak, star-lighted sky; the market people and other early stragglers, trotting to circulate their almost frozen blood; the hospitable light and warmth of the few coffee shops and public houses that were open for such customers; the hard, dry, frosty rime with which the air was charged (the wind had already beaten it into every crevice), and which lashed my face like a steel whip . . . I had resolved to make a visit to a certain spot (which I need not name) on the farther borders of Yorkshire . . . There was no Northern Railway at that time, and in its place there were stagecoaches; which I occasionally find myself, in common with some other people, affecting to lament now, but which everybody dreaded as a very serious penance then. I had secured the box-seat on the fastest of these, and my business in Fleet Street was to get into a cab with my portmanteau, so to make the best of my way to the Peacock at Islington,[48] where I was to join this coach. But when one of our Temple watchmen, who carried my portmanteau into Fleet Street for me, told me about the huge blocks of ice that had for some days past been floating in the river, having closed up in the night, and made a walk from the Temple Gardens over to the Surrey shore, I began to ask myself the question, whether the box-seat would not be likely to put a sudden and a frosty end to my unhappiness. I was heart-broken, it is true, and yet I was not quite so far gone as to

[48]   The Peacock Inn, formerly a public house on Islington High Street.

wish to be frozen to death. When I got up to the Peacock, where I found everybody drinking hot purl,[49] in self-preservation, I asked if there were an inside seat to spare. I then discovered that, inside or out, I was the only passenger. This gave me a still livelier idea of the great inclemency of the weather, since that coach always loaded particularly well. However, I took a little purl (which I found uncommonly good), and got into the coach. When I was seated, they built me up with straw to the waist, and, conscious of making a rather ridiculous appearance, I began my journey.[50]

Lord, how wearying it must have been for Mary, your mother, to trek from Nazareth to Bethlehem: a woman in the third trimester of pregnancy with only, probably, a donkey as transport.[51] Arduous and difficult, and yet, Lord, all part of your incarnation: no comfort zone loopholes on account of your divinity, but, truly, the Christ of the human road.

Jesus our brother, strong and good,
Was humbly born in a stable rude,
And the friendly beasts around him stood,
Jesus our brother, strong and good.
'I,' said the donkey, shaggy and brown,
'I carried His mother up hill and down
I carried her safely to Bethlehem town;
I,' said the donkey, shaggy and brown.[52]

[49] Purl (wormwood ale), infused with the tops of species of Artemisia which grows in coastal salt marsh.
[50] *The Holly Tree.*
[51] The popular donkey narrative stems from the fact that in ancient times, donkeys were a common mode of transportation, due to their gentle nature and ability to navigate rough terrain.
[52] From the c.twelfth-century French carol *The friendly beasts*, translated by Robert Davis (1881-1950).

**Better is one day in your courts than a thousand elsewhere;
I would rather be a doorkeeper in the house of my God than
dwell in the tents of the wicked.
(Psalm 84:10 NIV)**

He was a ticket-porter, Toby Veck, and waited there [just outside the church door] for jobs. And a breezy, goose-skinned, blue-nosed, red-eyed, stony-toed, tooth-chattering place it was, to wait in, in the winter-time, as Toby Veck well knew. The wind came tearing round the corner, especially the east wind, as if it had sallied forth, express, from the confines of the earth, to have a blow at Toby. And oftentimes it seemed to come upon him sooner than it had expected, for bouncing round the corner, and passing Toby, it would suddenly wheel round again, as if it cried 'Why, here he is!' Incontinently[53] his little white apron would be caught up over his head like a naughty boy's garments, and his feeble little cane would be seen to wrestle and struggle unavailingly in his hand, and his legs would undergo tremendous agitation, and Toby himself all aslant, and facing now in this direction, now in that, would be so banged and buffeted, and tousled, and worried, and hustled, and lifted off his feet, as to render it a state of things but one degree removed from a positive miracle, that he wasn't carried up bodily into the air as a colony of frogs or snails or other very portable creatures sometimes are, and rained down again, to the great astonishment of the natives, on some strange corner of the world where ticket-porters are unknown.[54]

---

[53] Old meaning: 'wanting self-restraint'.
[54] *The Chimes*.

Lord of the Church, how underrated and overlooked, all too often (forgive us), is the ministry of those who care for church buildings; who look after car parks, for example, keeping weeds at bay so that our premises don't become scruffy and unkempt, making for a bad witness. Thank you for those who tidy up, who arrange chairs, those who make sure the preacher has a glass of water to hand. Thank you for those who keep us supplied with toilet rolls, who brush away the cobwebs, and those who take the smelly bins out. Thank you, Lord, for those whose unsung ways mean we can use our churches and church halls, knowing they will be in good repair. Where would we be without the Toby Vecks of this world, keeping watch just by the church door.

They entered then the hallowed cave
Jesum hic adoraverunt,[55]
The best of all they had they gave,
Puerumque oraverunt,[56]
Pardon for that was lacking crave;
Subitoque abierunt.[57] [58]

[55] 'They worshipped Jesus here.'
[56] 'And the child prayed.'
[57] 'And suddenly they were gone.'
[58] From the carol *Come let us all sweet carols sing*, translated by Henry Ramsden Bramley (1833-1917), English clergyman and hymnologist.

The Word became flesh and made his dwelling among us.
(John 1:14 NIV)

The curtains of his bed were drawn aside; and Scrooge, starting up into a half-recumbent attitude, found himself face to face with the unearthly visitor who drew them: as close to it as I am now to you, and I am standing in the spirit at your elbow. It was a strange figure; like a child: yet not so like a child as like an old man, viewed through some supernatural medium, which gave him the appearance of having receded from the view, and being diminished to a child's proportions. Its hair, which hung about its neck and down its back, was white as if with age; and yet the face had not a wrinkle in it, and the tenderest bloom was on the skin. The arms were very long and muscular; the hands the same, as if its hold were of uncommon strength. Its legs and feet, most delicately formed, were, like those upper members, bare. It wore a tunic of the purest white; and round its waist was bound a lustrous belt, the sheen of which was beautiful. It held a branch of fresh green holly in its hand; and, in singular contradiction of that wintry emblem, had its dress trimmed with summer flowers. But the strangest thing about it was, that from the crown of its head there sprung a bright clear jet of light, by which all this was visible; and which was doubtless the occasion of its using, in its duller moments, a great extinguisher for a cap, which it now held under its arm. Even this, though, when Scrooge looked at it with increasing steadiness, was *not* its strangest quality. For as its belt sparkled and glittered now in one part and now in another, and what was light one instant, at another time was dark, so the figure itself fluctuated in its distinctness: being now a thing with one arm, now with one leg, now with twenty legs, now a pair of legs without a head, now a head without a body: of which dissolving parts, no outline would be visible in the dense gloom wherein they melted away. And in the very wonder of this, it would be itself again; distinct and clear as ever.[59]

I wonder what heaven might be like, Lord? The celestial city, the heavenly realm? Will it be anything like all I have known here on earth, or somewhere mysterious and strange? Will the life to come even bear any comparison to the only life I have known thus far? Will it take me a while to adjust, once I have parted with all that is familiar? I have no way of knowing, Lord Jesus, except to trust you with all that is yet to be experienced, and to believe wholeheartedly in your abiding presence within those eternal courts. And, that, Lord, is sufficient: to know that you will be there, to welcome, to guide, to keep, and to give your angels charge of my soul. I need not fear, for perfect love will surround me; and all because you came to Bethlehem to dwell among us and show the way. All will be well.

And our eyes at last shall see him,
Through his own redeeming love;
For that child, so dear and gentle,
Is our Lord in heaven above;
And he leads his children on
To the place where he is gone.[60]

---

[59] *A Christmas Carol.*
[60] From *Once in royal David's city.*

**If we have food and clothing, we will be content with that.
(1 Timothy 6:8 NIV)**

'Could I,' said Rosa, rising, as he jerked out of his chair in his ungainly way: 'could I ask you, most kindly to come to me at Christmas, if I had anything particular to say to you?' 'Why, certainly, certainly,' he rejoined; apparently – if such a word can be used of one who had no apparent lights or shadows about him – complimented by the question. 'As a particularly Angular man, I do not fit smoothly into the social circle, and consequently I have no other engagement at Christmas-time than to partake, on the twenty-fifth, of a boiled turkey and celery sauce with a – with a particularly Angular clerk I have the good fortune to possess, whose father, being a Norfolk farmer, sends him up (the turkey up), as a present to me, from the neighbourhood of Norwich. I should be quite proud of your wishing to see me, my dear. As a professional Receiver of rents, so very few people do wish to see me, that the novelty would be bracing.' For his ready acquiescence, the grateful Rosa put her hands upon his shoulders, stood on tiptoe, and instantly kissed him. 'Lord bless me!' cried Mr. Grewgious. 'Thank you, my dear! The honour is almost equal to the pleasure.'[61]

Thank you, Heavenly Father, for those, like the 'Norfolk farmer', who work hard to provide food for those of us who (if we are honest) sometimes take it for granted. This year, as we feast on a traditional Christmas dinner, or perhaps a vegetarian or vegan alternative, prompt us to give thanks for each person

[61]   *The Mystery of Edwin Drood.*

whose labour is represented on our tables; farm workers, factory employees, delivery drivers, shopkeepers, and so on. Prompt us, too, Lord, to bear in mind today's Bible verse.

Bring us out a table,
And spread it with a cloth;
Bring us out a mouldy cheese,[62]
And some of your Christmas loaf.[63]

---

[62] Ripened.
[63] From *The Wassail Song*.

**The virgin will conceive and give birth to a son,
and they will call him Immanuel
(which means 'God with us').
(Matthew 1:23 NIV)**

We had a friend who was our friend from early days, with whom we often pictured the changes that were to come upon our lives, and merrily imagined how we would speak, and walk, and think, and talk, when we came to be old. His destined habitation in the City of the Dead received him in his prime. Shall he be shut out from our Christmas remembrance? Would his love have so excluded us? Lost friend, lost child, lost parent, sister, brother, husband, wife, we will not so discard you! You shall hold your cherished places in our Christmas hearts, and by our Christmas fires; and in the season of immortal hope, and on the birthday of immortal mercy, we will shut out Nothing! The winter sun goes down over town and village; on the sea it makes a rosy path, as if the sacred tread were fresh upon the water. A few more moments, and it sinks, and night comes on, and lights begin to sparkle in the prospect. On the hillside beyond the shapelessly-diffused town, and in the quiet keeping of the trees that gird the village steeple, remembrances are cut in stone, planted in common flowers, growing in grass, entwined with lowly brambles around many a mound of earth. In town and village, there are doors and windows closed against the weather, there are flaming logs heaped high, there are joyful faces, there is healthy music of voices. Be all ungentleness and harm excluded from the temples of the household gods, but be those remembrances admitted with tender encouragement![64]

---

[64]   *What Christmas is as we grow older.*

Lord Jesus, look with pity and compassion upon all those whose Christmas and New Year is tinged with the sadness and remembrance of loss, and all the tumbling emotions that join with that sorrow, however old or however fresh (and raw) that might be. Christmases and new years are, inevitably, as we grow older, touched by grief. Memories of those gone before are obliged to mingle with all the sparkle and gaiety of the season. It's not an easy combination to manage, Lord. Such heartache seems incongruous; at odds with all that is so very happy. Man of Sorrows, as we celebrate, draw close to those who also commemorate. Gently soothe their pain as they remember those who hold 'cherished places in our Christmas hearts'. Be with us, Immanuel. Be with them.

In the bleak mid-winter
Frosty wind made moan
Earth stood hard as iron,
Water like a stone;
Snow had fallen, snow on snow,
Snow on snow.
In the bleak mid-winter
Long ago.[65]

[65] From the carol of the same name, by Christina Rossetti (1830-1894), writer of children's poetry, romantic poetry, and carols.

**He had no beauty or majesty to attract us to him,
nothing in his appearance that we should desire him.
(Isaiah 53:2 NIV)**

I live in a lodging in the Clapham Road, a very clean back room, in a very respectable house, where I am expected not to be at home in the day-time, unless poorly; and which I usually leave in the morning at nine o'clock, on pretence of going to business. I take my breakfast; my roll and butter, and my half-pint of coffee, at the old-established coffee shop near Westminster Bridge; and then I go into the City, I don't know why, and sit in Garraway's Coffee House, and on 'Change,[66] and walk about, and look into a few offices and counting-houses where some of my relations or acquaintance are so good as to tolerate me, and where I stand by the fire if the weather happens to be cold. I get through the day in this way until five o'clock, and then I dine: at a cost, on the average, of one and threepence. Having still a little money to spend on my evening's entertainment, I look into the old-established coffee shop as I go home, and take my cup of tea, and perhaps my bit of toast. So, as the large hand of the clock makes its way round to the morning hour again, I make my way round to the Clapham Road again, and go to bed when I get to my lodging, fire being expensive, and being objected to by the family on account of its giving trouble and making a dirt. Sometimes, one of my relations or acquaintances is so obliging as to ask me to dinner. Those are holiday occasions, and then I generally walk in the park. I am a solitary man, and seldom walk with anybody. Not that I am avoided because I am shabby; for I am not at all shabby, having always a very good suit of black

[66] The Stock Exchange.

on (or rather Oxford mixture, which has the appearance of black and wears much better); but I have got into a habit of speaking low, and being rather silent, and my spirits are not high, and I am sensible that I am not an attractive companion.[67]

Lord, there is something terribly poignant about that statement: 'I am sensible that I am not an attractive companion.' It seems so horrible. Yet, it is the lot of many to spend their time – hours, days, weeks, even – on their own. Loneliness is a silent blight upon what we imagine to be a civilised culture, Lord, when, through no particular fault of their own, multitudes of people have no-one but themselves for company, day in and day out. What a crushing burden that is, perhaps even more so when Christmas festivities are based around family and friendships. Lord Jesus, our Bible text today reminds us that you knew (and know) all about this; you knew only too well the weight of being an outcast. Unwanted God, bless those who are lonely this day.

Be near me, Lord Jesus
I ask thee to stay
Close by me forever
And love me I pray.[68]

[67] *The Poor Relation's Story.*
[68] From the carol *Away in a manger*, attributed to Martin Luther (1483-1546), German priest and theologian, Anonymous, and John Thomas McFarland (1852-1913), American pastor and advocate of Sunday schools. This carol appears to be a collaboration of verses and translations, with no fixed authorship.

You, Bethlehem Ephrathah, though you are small among the clans of Judah, out of you will come for me one who will be ruler over Israel.
(Micah 5:2 NIV)

When we came in sight of a town, it looked, to my fancy, like a large drawing on a slate, with abundance of slate-pencil expended on the churches and houses where the snow lay thickest. When we came within a town, and found the church clocks all stopped, the dial-faces choked with snow, and the inn signs blotted out, it seemed as if the whole place were overgrown with white moss. As to the coach, it was a mere snowball; similarly, the men and boys who ran along beside us to the town's end, turning our clogged wheels and encouraging our horses, were men and boys of snow; and the bleak wild solitude to which they at last dismissed us was a snowy Sahara. One would have thought this enough: notwithstanding which, I pledge my word that it snowed and snowed, and still it snowed, and never left off snowing. We performed Auld Lang Syne the whole day; seeing nothing, out of towns and villages, but the track of stoats, hares, and foxes, and sometimes of birds. At nine o'clock at night, on a Yorkshire moor, a cheerful burst from our horn, and a welcome sound of talking, with a glimmering and moving about of lanterns, roused me from my drowsy state. I found that we were going to change. They helped me out, and I said to a waiter, whose bare head became as white as King Lear's in a single minute, 'What inn is this?' 'The Holly Tree, sir,' said he. 'Upon my word, I believe,' said I, apologetically, to the guard and coachman, 'that I must stop here.'[69]

[69]   *The Holly Tree.*

It's true, Lord, that relatively insignificant places can make a lasting impression upon our lives; a birthplace, for example, or somewhere that carries memorable significance; a childhood home, maybe. The place itself doesn't need to be well known or even especially picturesque. It can be, as in this instance, a building or a setting that represents circumstances recalled with gratitude and affection. Maybe, like The Holly Tree Inn, an unremarkable premises, but a destination remembered, nevertheless, for providing warmth and welcome when it was most needed, or a modest church building, perhaps, wherein a spiritual encounter took place. Thank you, Lord, for landmarks on our journey. Help us to pause to meet (or remember) you there.

❧ ——— ☙

God bless the master of this house,
Likewise the mistress too;
And all the little children
That round the table go.[70]

---

[70] From *The wassail song* or *Here we come a-wassailing*. This dates from the nineteenth century, but is probably much older. It is thought to be one of the earliest carols sung door-to-door. Authorship uncertain.

**Let us then approach God's throne of grace with
confidence, so that we may receive mercy and find grace.
(Hebrews 4:16 NIV)**

The lady lifts her veil, and shows a face no older than the nurse's. A face far more refined and capable than hers, but wild and worn with sorrow. 'I am the miserable mother of a baby lately received under your care. I have a prayer to make to you.' Instinctively respecting the confidence which has drawn aside the veil, Sally, whose ways are all ways of simplicity and spontaneity, replaces it, and begins to cry. 'You will listen to my prayer?' the lady urges. 'You will not be deaf to the agonised entreaty of such a broken suppliant as I am?' 'O dear, dear, dear!' cries Sally. 'What shall I say, or can say! Don't talk of prayers. Prayers are to be put up to the Good Father of All, and not to nurses and such. And there! I am only to hold my place for half a year longer, till another young woman can be trained up to it. I am going to be married. I shouldn't have been out last night, and I shouldn't have been out to-night, but that my Dick (he is the young man I am going to be married to) lies ill, and I help his mother and sister to watch him. Don't take on so, don't take on so!' 'O good Sally, dear Sally,' moans the lady, catching at her dress entreatingly. 'As you are hopeful, and I am hopeless; as a fair way in life is before you, which can never, never, be before me; as you can aspire to become a respected wife, and as you can aspire to become a proud mother, as you are a living loving woman, and must die; for GOD'S sake hear my distracted petition!'[71]

---

[71] *No Thoroughfare.*

'You will listen to my prayer?' O, Lord, don't we complicate prayer! We try this way and that, we give up, we lapse, we falsely imagine we need to be in a certain state of mind before you will grant us a hearing, we feel we cannot possibly approach you until we get our act together, when all the time, you are more than willing to listen: we are on standing invitation to 'put up' our prayers 'to the Good Father of All.' Heavenly Father, teach us of your merciful willingness to attend to our petitions, for we are not dealing with a reluctant God. Help us to pray just as we are; heart to heart, without pretence or polish, and to find your throne of grace as accessible as ever. After all, Lord Jesus, one of the great beauties of your Bethlehem incarnation is that you came to open up glorious lines of direct communication between us and all that heaven has to offer. Not only that, you intercede for us; we don't even pray alone. As we bring our distracted petitions, teach us how to pray. This season, of all seasons, may we each, afresh, 'draw near to God'.

Then entered in those wise men three
Full reverently upon their knee,
And offered there in his presence
Their gold, and myrrh and frankincense.
Noel, noel, noel, noel!
Born is the King of Israel![72]

---

[72] From *We three kings of orient are.*

Provide the poor wanderer with shelter.
(Isaiah 58:7 NIV)

RICHARD WATTS, Esq. by his Will, dated 22 Aug. 1579, founded this Charity for Six poor Travellers, who not being ROGUES, or PROCTORS, May receive gratis for one Night, Lodging, Entertainment, and Fourpence each.[73]

It was in the ancient little city of Rochester in Kent, of all the good days in the year upon a Christmas Eve, that I stood reading this inscription over the quaint old door in question. I had been wandering about the neighbouring cathedral, and had seen the tomb of Richard Watts, with the effigy of worthy Master Richard starting out of it like a ship's figure-head; and I had felt that I could do no less, as I gave the verger his fee, than inquire the way to Watts's Charity. The way being very short and very plain, I had come prosperously to the inscription and the quaint old door ... I found it to be a clean white house, of a staid and venerable air, with the quaint old door already three times mentioned (an arched door), choice little long low lattice-windows, and a roof of three gables . . . While I was yet surveying it with growing content, I espied, at one of the upper lattices which stood open, a decent body, of a wholesome matronly appearance, whose eyes I caught inquiringly addressed to mine. They said so plainly, 'Do you wish to see the house?' that I answered aloud, 'Yes, if you please.' And within a minute the old door opened, and I bent my head, and went down two steps into the entry. 'This,' said the matronly presence, ushering me into a low room on the right, 'is where the

[73] Following his death in 1579, Richard Watts Charity was established, and still works in Rochester, providing alms-house accommodation, grants, and home help services.

travellers sit by the fire, and cook what bits of suppers they buy with their fourpences.' 'O! Then they have no entertainment?' said I. For the inscription over the outer door was still running in my head, and I was mentally repeating, in a kind of tune, 'Lodging, entertainment, and fourpence each.' 'They have a fire provided for 'em,' returned the matron; a mighty civil person, not, as I could make out, overpaid; 'and these cooking utensils. And this what's painted on a board is the rules for their behaviour. They have their fourpences when they get their tickets from the steward over the way, for I don't admit 'em myself, they must get their tickets first, and sometimes one buys a rasher of bacon, and another a herring, and another a pound of potatoes, or what not. Sometimes two or three of 'em will club their fourpences together, and make a supper that way. But not much of anything is to be got for fourpence, at present, when provisions is so dear.'[74]

Lord, in your mercy, bless those of no fixed abode, who rely on the kindness of friends and strangers for shelter and sustenance.

The night before that happy day of grace
The Virgin mother had no resting place:
She and her pious Joseph were so low
They knew not whither or which to go.
For they were forced to wander up and down,
And could not find a lodging in the town;
But in an ox's stall where beasts are fed
The mother of our Lord was brought to bed.[75]

---

[74] *The Seven Poor Travellers.*
[75] From the carol *The black decree.* Date and authorship uncertain.

**One day Elisha went to Shunem. And a well-to-do woman was
there, who urged him to stay for a meal. So whenever
he came by, he stopped there to eat. She said to her husband,
'I know that this man who often comes our way is a holy man
of God. Let's make a small room on the roof and put in
it a bed and a table, a chair and a lamp for him.
Then he can stay there whenever he comes to us'.
(2 Kings 4:8-10 NIV)**

I had been looking about the room, admiring its snug fireside at
the upper end, its glimpse of the street through the low mullioned
window, and its beams overhead. 'It is very comfortable,' said I.
'Ill-convenient,'[76] observed the matronly presence. I liked to hear
her say so; for it showed a commendable anxiety to execute in no
niggardly spirit the intentions of Master Richard Watts. But the
room was really so well adapted to its purpose that I protested,
quite enthusiastically, against her disparagement. 'Nay, ma'am,'
said I, 'I am sure it is warm in winter and cool in summer. It has a
look of homely welcome and soothing rest. It has a remarkably cosy
fireside, the very blink of which, gleaming out into the street upon
a winter night, is enough to warm all Rochester's heart. And as to
the convenience of the six Poor Travellers —' 'I don't mean them,'
returned the presence. 'I speak of its being an ill-convenience to
myself and my daughter, having no other room to sit in of a night.'
This was true enough, but there was another quaint room of
corresponding dimensions on the opposite side of the entry: so
I stepped across to it, through the open doors of both rooms, and
asked what this chamber was for. 'This,' returned the presence,
'is the Board Room. Where the gentlemen meet when they

[76] Throughout the original narrative, 'convenient' is spelt 'conwenient' but is
altered here for easier reading.

come here.' Let me see. I had counted from the street six upper windows besides these on the ground storey. Making a perplexed calculation in my mind, I rejoined, 'Then the six poor travellers sleep upstairs?' My new friend shook her head. 'They sleep,' she answered, 'in two little outer galleries at the back, where their beds has always been, ever since the charity was founded. It being so very ill-convenient to me as things is at present, the gentlemen are going to take off a bit of the back-yard, and make a slip of a room for 'em there, to sit in before they go to bed.'[77]

Lord, if I may be honest, I don't always enjoy being put to any inconvenience. I enjoy my little ways and routines. Forgive me, especially if I am sometimes reluctant to trouble myself for the sake of your work, when you ask me to go the second mile. Help me, Lord, to consider any inconveniences a small price to pay in your service. Turn my reluctance to readiness.

Light of the everlasting morn,
Deep through my spirit shine;
There let thy presence newly born
Make all my being thine;
There try me as the silver, try,
And cleanse my soul with care
Till thou art able to descry
Thy faultless image there.[78]

---

[77] *The Seven Poor Travellers.*
[78] From the carol *'Twas in the winter cold* by Charles Ingham Black (c.1821-c.1896), Sligo-born priest, theologian and scholar.

Mary said: 'My soul glorifies the Lord'.
(Luke 1:46 NIV)

I had never seen such a large room as that into which they showed me. It had five windows, with dark red curtains that would have absorbed the light of a general illumination; and there were complications of drapery at the top of the curtains, that went wandering about the wall in a most extraordinary manner. I asked for a smaller room, and they told me there was no smaller room. They could screen me in, however, the landlord said. They brought a great old japanned screen, with natives (Japanese, I suppose) engaged in a variety of idiotic pursuits all over it; and left me roasting whole before an immense fire. My bedroom was some quarter of a mile off, up a great staircase at the end of a long gallery; and nobody knows what a misery this is to a bashful man who would rather not meet people on the stairs. It was the grimmest room I have ever had the nightmare in; and all the furniture, from the four posts of the bed to the two old silver candlesticks, was tall, high-shouldered, and spindle-waisted. Below, in my sitting-room, if I looked round my screen, the wind rushed at me like a mad bull; if I stuck to my armchair, the fire scorched me to the colour of a new brick. The chimney-piece was very high and … if I stood with my back to the fire, a gloomy vault of darkness above and beyond the screen insisted on being looked at; and, in its dim remoteness, the drapery of the ten curtains of the five windows went twisting and creeping about, like a nest of gigantic worms. I suppose that what I observe in myself must be observed by some other men of similar character in *themselves*; therefore I am emboldened to mention, that, when I travel, I never arrive at a place but I immediately want to go away from it. Before I had finished my supper of broiled fowl and mulled port, I had impressed upon the waiter in detail my arrangements for departure in the morning.[79]

That's a detail to ponder, Lord: how others might see me, and what they might observe in my conduct. At this time of year, when your name, Lord Jesus, is sung in any number of Christmas carols, and heard across the airwaves as the story of your birth is given seasonal prominence, help me, I pray, to bear good witness to that which I profess. May aspects of your character within me only ever serve to reinforce the message shared by countless churches in these days, so that what is heard is also 'observed by some' as you live in me.

Teach, o teach us, holy child,
By thy face so meek and mild,
Teach us to resemble thee,
In thy sweet humility.[80]

---

[79]   *The Holly Tree.*
[80]   From the carol *See amid the winter's snow* (also known as *Hymn for Christmas Day*) by Edward Caswell (1814–1878), Anglican clergyman who converted to Roman Catholicism.

**A son, a male child, who 'will rule all the nations
with an iron sceptre'.
(Revelation 12:5 NIV)**

As brisk as bees, if not altogether as light as fairies, did the four Pickwickians assemble on the morning of the twenty-second day of December, in the year of grace in which these, their faithfully-recorded adventures, were undertaken and accomplished. Christmas was close at hand, in all his bluff and hearty honesty; it was the season of hospitality, merriment, and open-heartedness; the old year was preparing, like an ancient philosopher, to call his friends around him, and amidst the sound of feasting and revelry to pass gently and calmly away. Gay and merry was the time; and right gay and merry were at least four of the numerous hearts that were gladdened by its coming. And numerous indeed are the hearts to which Christmas brings a brief season of happiness and enjoyment. How many families, whose members have been dispersed and scattered far and wide, in the restless struggles of life, are then reunited, and meet once again in that happy state of companionship and mutual

goodwill, which is a source of such pure and unalloyed delight; and one so incompatible with the cares and sorrows of the world, that the religious belief of the most civilised nations, and the rude traditions of the roughest savages, alike number it among the first joys of a future condition of existence, provided for the blessed and happy! How many old recollections, and how many dormant sympathies, does Christmas time awaken![81]

Lord Jesus, I pray today for those who, this Christmas, will be overseas, separated from family, loved ones, and friends. I pray too for those working with Christian missions in lands where the message of Christmas means very little, and is mingled with stories of Father Christmas and snowmen; a peculiar amalgam of myth and cultural misappropriation. Maybe it's unlikely that missionary workers nowadays will encounter 'the roughest savages' but even so, the good news of your incarnation still needs to be imparted against a backdrop of misunderstanding. Bless their work, and bless all who shan't be home this year.

Joy to the world, the Lord is come,
Let earth receive her King;
Let every heart prepare him room,
And heaven and nature sing.

He rules the world with truth and grace,
And makes the nations prove,
The glories of his righteousness,
And wonders of his love.[82]

---

[81] *The Pickwick Papers.*

[82] From the carol of the same name by Isaac Watts (1674-1748), a minister in the Independent Church and a prolific writer/lyricist.

This is eternal life: that they know you, the only true God, and Jesus Christ, whom you have sent.
(John 17:3 NIV)

We write these words now, many miles distant from the spot at which, year after year, we met on that day, a merry and joyous circle. Many of the hearts that throbbed so gaily then, have ceased to beat; many of the looks that shone so brightly then, have ceased to glow; the hands we grasped, have grown cold; the eyes we sought, have hid their lustre in the grave; and yet the old house, the room, the merry voices and smiling faces, the jest, the laugh, the most minute and trivial circumstances connected with those happy meetings, crowd upon our mind at each recurrence of the season, as if the last assemblage had been but yesterday! Happy, happy Christmas, that can win us back to the delusions of our childish days; that can recall to the old man the pleasures of his youth; that can transport the sailor and the traveller, thousands of miles away, back to his own fireside and his quiet home![83]

How all-too-quickly, Lord, the years seem to pass. Everything Charles Dickens says here rings so very true: we reflect, and sometimes it all seems as if so many treasured memories 'had been but yesterday.' And, yet, Lord, even with the gift of three score years and ten, our time here is as nothing compared to an unimaginable eternity. As important and as lovely and as varied as these days are, and forasmuch as I thank you for the wonderful opportunity of living life in all its fullness, help me, I pray, to live, too, with eternal life in mind. Shape my heart around that reality,

[83]   *The Pickwick Papers.*

that I may prepare well, in the here and now, for the hereafter.
Thank you, Heavenly Father, for sending Jesus; your Son, my
Saviour.

Good Christians all, rejoice,
With heart and soul and voice!
Hear the news of endless bliss,
Jesus Christ was born for this:
He has opened heaven's door
And man is blessed for evermore!
Christ was born for this;
Christ was born for this.[84]

[84] From the carol of the same name by John Mason Neale.

**Beyond all question, the mystery from which true
godliness springs is great.
(1 Timothy 3:16 NIV)**

Christmas Eve in Cloisterham. A few strange faces in the streets; a few other faces, half strange and half familiar, once the faces of Cloisterham children, now the faces of men and women who come back from the outer world at long intervals to find the city wonderfully shrunken in size, as if it had not washed by any means well in the meanwhile. To these, the striking of the cathedral clock, and the cawing of the rooks from the cathedral tower, are like voices of their nursery time. To such as these, it has happened in their dying hours afar off, that they have imagined their chamber floor to be strewn with the autumnal leaves fallen from the elm trees in the Close: so have the rustling sounds and fresh scents of their earliest impressions revived when the circle of their lives was very nearly traced, and the beginning and the end were drawing close together.[85]

Thank you, Lord, for the touches of mystery that float gently between these lines; of smells and senses, memories and imaginings, and that which is 'very nearly traced.' Preserve that element of the divinely mysterious in my walk with you, I pray. May it be a component of faith that delivers me from the tyranny of having to understand and dissect everything. Rather, let me be comfortable with that which I cannot comprehend, grasp, or know, for in my not knowing, I acknowledge something of your greatness, ineffable God.

[85]   *The Mystery of Edwin Drood.*

O magnum mysterium,
Et admirabile sacramentum,
Et animalia viderent Dominum natum,
Iacentem in praesepio!
O beata virgo, cuius viscera
Meruerunt portare
Dominum Iesum Christum.
Alleluia![86]

O great mystery,
And wonderful sacrament,
That animals should see the newborn Lord,
Lying in a manger!
O blessed virgin, whose womb
Was worthy to bear
The Lord Jesus Christ.
Alleluia![87]

[86]   Original Latin.
[87]   From *The Matins of Christmas* in *The Roman Breviary*, a Roman Catholic liturgical book containing prayers, hymns, the Psalms, readings, and notations.

They saw the child with his mother Mary, and they bowed down and worshipped him. Then they opened their treasures and presented him with gifts of gold, frankincense and myrrh. (Matthew 2:11 NIV)

Seasonable tokens are about. Red berries shine here and there in the lattices of Minor Canon Corner; Mr and Mrs Tope are daintily sticking sprigs of holly into the carvings and sconces of the cathedral stalls, as if they were sticking them into the coat-button-holes of the Dean and Chapter. Lavish profusion is in the shops: particularly in the articles of currants, raisins, spices, candied peel, and moist sugar. An unusual air of gallantry and dissipation is abroad; evinced in an immense bunch of mistletoe hanging in the greengrocer's shop doorway, and a poor little Twelfth Cake,[88] culminating in the figure of a Harlequin – such a very poor little Twelfth Cake, that one would rather call it a Twenty-fourth Cake or a Forty-eighth Cake – to be raffled for at the pastry cook's, terms one shilling per member. Public amusements are not wanting. The waxwork which made so deep an impression on the reflective mind of the Emperor of China is to be seen by particular desire during Christmas Week only, on the premises of the bankrupt livery-stable-keeper up the lane; and a new grand comic Christmas pantomime is to be produced at the theatre: the latter heralded by the portrait of Signor Jacksonini the clown, saying 'How do you do tomorrow?' quite as large as life, and almost as miserably. In short, Cloisterham is up and doing.[89]

---

[88] Or Twelfth Night Cake, a medieval tradition: a large fruit cake to celebrate the Twelfth Night of Epiphany.
[89] *The Mystery of Edwin Drood.*

Signs and symbols, Lord; 'seasonable tokens' of commemoration – those markers by which we note specials occasions. Such visible elements of faith and worship are of course more important to some than others; icons, ornate crucifixes, and paintings. For many believers, they are helpful aids to devotion and adoration. I pray, Lord, for my brothers and sisters in Christ whose denominational bias leans towards the elaborate and ceremonial. I ask your rich blessing upon them, just as much as I pray equal blessings upon my fellow Christians whose celebrations tend to be much more low-key. Come to us each in mercy and grace. We're all seeking the same Saviour.

There were three wise men from afar
Directed by a glorious star,
And on they wandered night and day
Until they came where Jesus lay,
And when they came unto that place
Where our beloved Messiah was,
They humbly cast them at his feet,
With gifts of gold and incense sweet.[90]

---

[90]   From *The Wexford Carol*, an ancient Irish carol. Authorship uncertain.

**If we are faithless, he remains faithful,
for he cannot disown himself.
(2 Timothy 2:13 NIV)**

The year came round to Christmas–time, and I had been at home above two months. I had seen Agnes frequently. However loud the general voice might be in giving me encouragement, and however fervent the emotions and endeavours to which it roused me, I heard her lightest word of praise as I heard nothing else. At least once a week, and sometimes oftener, I rode over there, and passed the evening. I usually rode back at night; for the old unhappy sense was always hovering about me now, most sorrowfully when I left her, and I was glad to be up and out, rather than wandering over the past in weary wakefulness or miserable dreams. I wore away the longest part of many wild sad nights, in those rides; reviving, as I went, the thoughts that had occupied me in my long absence. Or, if I were to say rather that I listened to the echoes of those thoughts, I should better express the truth. They spoke to me from afar off. I had put them at a distance, and accepted my inevitable place. When I read to Agnes what I wrote; when I saw her listening face; moved her to smiles or tears; and heard her cordial voice so earnest on the shadowy events of that imaginative world in which I lived; I thought what a fate mine might have been, but only thought so, as I had thought after I was married to Dora, what I could have wished my wife to be. My duty to Agnes, who loved me with a love, which, if I disquieted, I wronged most selfishly and poorly, and could never restore; my matured assurance that I, who had worked out my own destiny, and won what I had impetuously set my heart on, had no right to murmur, and must bear; comprised what I felt and what I had learned. But I loved her: and now it even became some consolation to me, vaguely to conceive a distant day when I might blamelessly avow it; when all this should be over; when I could say 'Agnes, so it was when I came home; and now I am old, and I never have loved since!' She did not once show me any change in herself. What she always had been to me, she still was; wholly unaltered.[91]

A complicated story here, Lord, one of twists and turns and emotions pulled one way, and then another. How reminiscent this might be, Lord Jesus, of our dealings with you! We know well of your 'wholly unaltered' love for us. We know that what you have always been to us, you still are; entirely loving, faithful, and kind. Yet, we know, too, of our own fickle ways, when our love in return is sometimes selfish and poorly, arising from divided hearts. Have mercy, Lord, and forgive us. This Christmas-time, restore us to our rightful minds.

Thou art the very light of light,
Enlighten us, sweet child,
That we may keep thy birthday bright
With service undefiled.[92]

---

[91] *David Copperfield.*

[92] From the carol *Emmanuel, God with us* by William Chatterton Dix (1837-1898), English hymn-writer and the manager of a marine insurance company in Glasgow.

**A great army of heaven's angels appeared with the angel,
singing praises to God.
(Luke 2:13 GNB)**

Mrs. Joe was prodigiously busy in getting the house ready for the festivities of the day, and Joe had been put upon the kitchen doorstep to keep him out of the dustpan, an article into which his destiny always led him sooner or later, when my sister was vigorously reaping the floors of her establishment. 'And where the deuce ha' you been?' was Mrs. Joe's Christmas salutation, when I and my conscience showed ourselves. I said I had been down to hear the carols. 'Ah! well!' observed Mrs. Joe. 'You might ha' done worse.' Not a doubt of that, I thought. 'Perhaps if I warn't a blacksmith's wife, and (what's the same thing) a slave with her apron never off, I should have been to hear the carols,' said Mrs. Joe. 'I'm rather partial to carols, myself, and that's the best of reasons for my never hearing any.'[93]

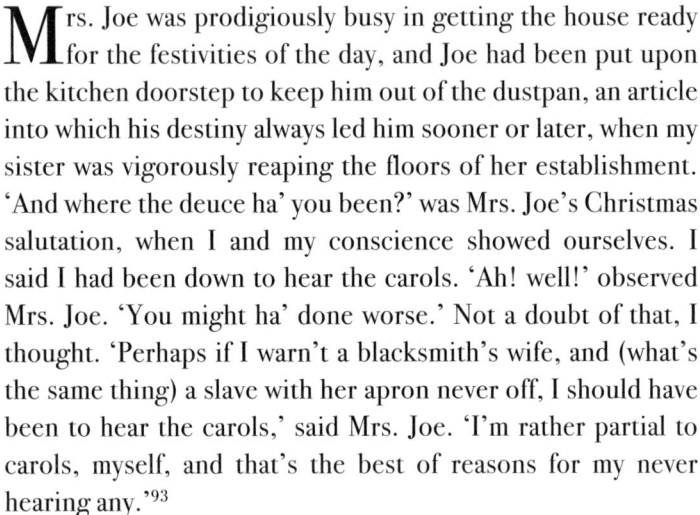

If familiarity breeds contempt, Lord, as it so often can, then I pray for that not to be the case this Christmas-time, when 'the carols' are sung in churches, on street corners, on doorsteps, and in radio or television broadcasts. Carols are saturated with theological meanings and echoes of love, Lord, and it would be sad if their true messages were ignored or not really taken in. I pray, as we listen, Lord, and as we sing, that you will touch our hearts afresh with the great truths of this season. Refresh our listening, and bring 'the carols' alive in a new way. I pray, too,

[93] *Great Expectations.*

for every 'Mrs. Joe' whose work and responsibilities prevent them from worshipping in any formal, collective sense. Make that blessing up to them.

And all the angels in heaven shall sing,
On Christmas Day, on Christmas Day;
And all the angels in heaven shall sing,
On Christmas Day in the morning.

And all the souls on earth shall sing,
On Christmas Day, on Christmas Day;
And all the souls on earth shall sing,
On Christmas Day in the morning.[94]

[94] From the carol *I saw three ships*, thought to have been published in the seventeenth century. Authorship uncertain.

Jesus called the children to him and said, 'Let the little children come to me, and do not hinder them, for the kingdom of God belongs to such as these. Truly I tell you, anyone who will not receive the kingdom of God like a little child will never enter it.'
(Luke 18:16, 17 NIV)

Mr. Wopsle, the clerk at church, was to dine with us; and Mr. Hubble the wheelwright and Mrs. Hubble; and Uncle Pumblechook (Joe's uncle, but Mrs. Joe appropriated him), who was a well-to-do corn-chandler in the nearest town, and drove his own chaise-cart. The dinner hour was half past one. When Joe and I got home, we found the table laid, and Mrs. Joe dressed, and the dinner dressing, and the front door unlocked (it never was at any other time) for the company to enter by, and everything most splendid . . . Mr. Wopsle said grace with theatrical declamation, as it now appears to me, something like a religious cross of the ghost in Hamlet with Richard the Third, and ended with the very proper aspiration that we might be truly grateful. Upon which my sister fixed me with her eye, and said, in a low reproachful voice, 'Do you hear that? Be grateful.' 'Especially,' said Mr. Pumblechook, 'be grateful, boy, to them which brought you up by hand.' Mrs. Hubble shook her head, and contemplating me with a mournful presentiment that I should come to no good, asked, 'Why is it that the young are never grateful?' This moral mystery seemed too much for the company until Mr. Hubble tersely solved it by saying, 'Naterally wicious.' Everybody then murmured 'True!' and looked at me in a particularly unpleasant and personal manner.[95]

---

[95]   *Great Expectations.*

A few prayers come to mind today, Lord: Protect me from the temptation to act as though I am in some way holier than others, for I am not. Likewise, deliver me from any inclination to judge anyone else, for I am not entitled to do so. Help me only ever to encourage and support any young people who come along to share church with me. Theirs is a complex world about which I know little, and my looking down on them won't help one single bit.

Come, nor fear to seek him, children though we be;
Once he said of children, 'Let them come to me.'

Fear not then to enter, though we cannot bring
Gold, or myrrh, or incense fitting for a King.

Gifts he asketh richer, offerings costlier still.
Yet may Christian children bring them if they will.[96]

[96] From the carol *Waken! Christian children* by Samuel Collingwood Hamerton (1833-1872), Vicar of St. Paul's, Warwick. There is some discrepancy about the place of his death; it was either Warwick or the Isle of Wight.

A cheerful heart is good medicine.
(Proverbs 17:22 NIV)

'Mrs. Joe,' said Uncle Pumblechook: a large, hard-breathing, middle-aged slow man, with a mouth like a fish, dull staring eyes, and sandy hair standing upright on his head, so that he looked as if he had just been all but choked, and had that moment come to; 'I have brought you, as the compliments of the season, I have brought you, Mum, a bottle of sherry wine, and I have brought you, Mum, a bottle of port wine.' Every Christmas Day he presented himself, as a profound novelty, with exactly the same words, and carrying the two bottles like dumbbells. Every Christmas Day, Mrs. Joe replied, as she now replied, 'Oh, Un — cle Pum — ble — chook! This IS kind!' Every Christmas Day, he retorted, as he now retorted, 'It's no more than your merits. And now are you all bobbish, and how's Sixpennorth of halfpence?' meaning me. We dined on these occasions in the kitchen, and adjourned, for the nuts and oranges and apples, to the parlour; which was a change very like Joe's change from his working clothes to his Sunday dress. My sister was uncommonly lively on the present occasion, and indeed was generally more gracious in the society of Mrs. Hubble than in other company. I remember Mrs. Hubble as a little curly sharp-edged person in sky blue, who held a conventionally juvenile position, because she had married Mr. Hubble, I don't know at what remote period, when she was much younger than he. I remember Mr Hubble as a tough high-shouldered stooping old man, of a sawdusty fragrance, with his legs extraordinarily wide apart: so that in my short days I always saw some miles of open country between them when I met him coming up the lane.[97]

[97]   *Great Expectations.*

Thank you, Lord, for these amusing glimpses into Charles Dickens' lovely sense of humour. Thank you for granting him the ability to describe people and situations in such comical ways, and for all who grace life with a capacity to see the funny side of things: they are a tonic. Thank you, Lord, for inventing and granting the gift of laughter. It's a great idea and it helps life along so much, perhaps especially when it pricks pomposity!

We wish you a merry Christmas,
We wish you a merry Christmas,
We wish you a merry Christmas
And a happy New Year.
Good tidings we bring
To you and your kin;
We wish you a merry Christmas
And a happy New Year.[98]

---

[98] Several versions of this carol have been produced over the years, but the original authorship is attributed to E.D. Gritman. No biographical information appears to exist.

Greet one another with a kiss of love.
(1 Peter 5:14 NIV)

From the centre of the ceiling of this kitchen, old Wardle had just suspended with his own hands a huge branch of mistletoe, and this same branch of mistletoe instantaneously gave rise to a scene of general and most delightful struggling and confusion; in the midst of which Mr. Pickwick with a gallantry which would have done honour to a descendant of Lady Tollimglower herself, took the old lady by the hand, led her beneath the mystic branch, and saluted her in all courtesy and decorum. The old lady submitted to this piece of practical politeness with all the dignity which befitted so important and serious a solemnity, but the younger ladies not being so thoroughly imbued with a superstitious veneration of the custom, or imagining that the value of a salute is very much enhanced if it cost a little trouble to obtain it, screamed and struggled, and ran into corners, and threatened and remonstrated, and did everything but leave the room, until some of the less adventurous gentlemen were on the point of desisting, when they all at once found it useless to resist any longer, and submitted to be kissed with a good grace. Mr. Winkle kissed the young lady with the black eyes, and Mr. Snodgrass kissed Emily; and Mr. Weller, not being particular about the form of being under the mistletoe, kissed Emma and the other female servants, just as he caught them.[99]

Maybe we are skating on seasonally thin ice here, Lord! On the one hand, a party game, and some harmless fun; mistletoe and merriment, and no more than that. On the other hand, though,

[99]   *The Pickwick Papers.*

Christmas traditions that might, possibly, have potential to become something else, to everyone's regret. Help us, Lord, to admit our frailty in the face of temptation, however innocuously that temptation might first make its appearance, and however holy we might think ourselves to be. We don't want to be Christian killjoys with a po-faced style of witnessing, but neither do we wish to be naïve. Meet us with grace and understanding.

Mountains, bow your heads majestic,
Lowly vales arise and sing;
See approach the Prince celestial!
Earth receive thy heavenly King.

Crowned with grace and understanding,
Branch divine of Jesse's stem;
God of knowledge, wisdom, power,
Heaven's most glorious diadem.[100]

[100] From the carol of the same title by William Hayman Cummings (1831-1915), English musician and organist at Waltham Abbey Church.

The angel assured her, 'Mary, you have nothing to fear. God has a surprise for you: You will become pregnant and give birth to a son and call his name Jesus'.
(Luke 1:30, 31 MSG)

As to the poor relations, they kissed everybody, not even excepting the plainer portion of the young-lady visitors, who, in their excessive confusion, ran right under the mistletoe, directly it was hung up, without knowing it! Wardle stood with his back to the fire, surveying the whole scene, with the utmost satisfaction . . . Now the screaming had subsided, and faces were in a glow and curls in a tangle, and Mr. Pickwick, after kissing the old lady as before-mentioned, was standing under the mistletoe, looking with a very pleased countenance on all that was passing around him, when the young lady with the black eyes, after a little whispering with the other young ladies, made a sudden dart forward, and, putting her arm round Mr. Pickwick's neck, saluted him affectionately on the left cheek; and before Mr. Pickwick distinctly knew what was the matter, he was surrounded by the whole body, and kissed by every one of them. It was a pleasant thing to see Mr. Pickwick in the centre of the group, now pulled this way, and then that, and first kissed on the chin and then on the nose, and then on the spectacles, and to hear the peals of laughter which were raised on every side; but it was a still more pleasant thing to see Mr. Pickwick, blinded shortly afterwards, with a silk-handkerchief, falling up against the wall, and scrambling into corners, and going through all the mysteries of blind-man's buff, with the utmost relish for the game, until at last he caught one of the poor relations; and then had to evade the blind-man himself, which he did with a nimbleness and agility that elicited the admiration and applause of all beholders.[101]

The element of surprise, Lord – that which catches us unawares! What a surprise, Lord Jesus, that you, God made man, should appear in a scruffy old cattle shed one day! What a surprise that you should choose such an unexpected and unlikely means of reaching out to humankind; the humblest approach imaginable. Today, Lord, I pray that you would surprise those I pray for, who do not yet know you as their Lord and Saviour. Catch them unawares by kissing their thoughts and their hearts with love and revelation. God of surprises!

The angel Gabriel from heaven came,
His wings as drifted snow, his eyes as flame:
'From God, all hail,' the angel said to Mary,
'Most highly favoured lady!' Gloria!

'Fear not, for you shall bear a holy child,
by him shall we to God be reconciled;
his name shall be Emmanuel, the long-foretold:
most highly favoured lady!' Gloria![102]

---

[101]   *The Pickwick Papers.*
[102]   From the carol of the same name by Sabine Baring-Gould (1834–1924), Anglican priest and prolific hymnwriter.

Turn to me and be gracious to me, for I am lonely.
(Psalm 26:16 NIV)

In the morning I found that it was snowing still, that it had snowed all night, and that I was snowed up. Nothing could get out of that spot on the moor, or could come at it, until the road had been cut out by labourers from the market-town. When they might cut their way to the Holly Tree [Inn] nobody could tell me. It was now Christmas Eve. I should have had a dismal Christmas-time of it anywhere, and consequently that did not so much matter; still, being snowed up was like dying of frost, a thing I had not bargained for. I felt very lonely. Yet I could no more have proposed to the landlord and landlady to admit me to their society (though I should have liked it, very much) than I could have asked them to present me with a piece of plate. Here my great secret, the real bashfulness of my character, is to be observed. Like most bashful men, I judge of other people as if they were bashful too. Besides being far too shamefaced to make the proposal myself, I really had a delicate misgiving that it would be in the last degree disconcerting to them.[103]

The lonely, Lord Jesus: those who are lonely because, for one reason or another, they are bashful and socially awkward, and for whom seasons like this one are loaded with anxiety. I pray for them, here and now. The lonely, Lord Jesus, whose world view is dominated and skewed by concerns about what others might think of them, and whose actions are crippled by such worries. In your mercy, hear my prayer.

[103]   *The Holly Tree.*

Angels and archangels
May have gathered there,
Cherubim and seraphim
Thronged the air;
But only his mother
In her maiden bliss
Worshipped the beloved
With a kiss.[104]

---

[104] From *In the bleak mid-winter.*

**Remember the former things, those of long ago.
(Isaiah 46:9 NIV)**

There was an inn in the cathedral town where I went to school . . . It was the inn where friends used to put up, and where we used to go to see parents, and to have salmon and fowls, and be tipped. It had an ecclesiastical sign, The Mitre, and a bar that seemed to be the next best thing to a bishopric, it was so snug. I loved the landlord's youngest daughter to distraction, but let that pass. It was in this inn that I was cried over by my rosy little sister, because I had acquired a black eye in a fight. And though she had been, that Holly Tree night, for many a long year where all tears are dried, The Mitre softened me yet.[105]

A shorter reflection today, Lord, yet somewhat poignant, nevertheless. Memories of bygone days drift into our lives, as is so often the case at Christmas and New Year. Likewise, recollections of childhood. Thank you, Lord, for the special gift of memory, whereby people and places continue to live on in our hearts, long after actual moments have passed. As I reflect, at this time of year, receive my warmest gratitude for all that remains precious.

> Should auld acquaintance be forgot,
> And never brought to mind?
> Should auld acquaintance be forgot,
> And auld lang syne?[106]

---

[105] *The Holly Tree.*
[106] From *Auld lang syne*, a Scots-language poem written by Robert 'Rabbie' Burns (1759-1796), based on an older folk song. A reasonable translation of 'auld lang syne' would be 'old long since' or something like that.

The Lord is close to the brokenhearted.
(Psalm 34:18 NIV)

'To be continued to-morrow,' said I, when I took my candle to go to bed. But my bed took it upon itself to continue the train of thought that night. It carried me away, like the enchanted carpet, to a distant place (though still in England), and there, alighting from a stage-coach at another inn in the snow, as I had actually done some years before, I repeated in my sleep a curious experience I had really had there. More than a year before I made the journey in the course of which I put up at that inn, I had lost a very near and dear friend by death. Every night since, at home or away from home, I had dreamed of that friend; sometimes as still living; sometimes as returning from the world of shadows to comfort me; always as being beautiful, placid, and happy, never in association with any approach to fear or distress. It was at a lonely inn in a wide moorland place, that I halted to pass the night. When I had looked from my bedroom window over the waste of snow on which the moon was shining, I sat down by my fire to write a letter. I had always, until that hour, kept it within my own breast that I dreamed every night of the dear lost one. But in the letter that I wrote I recorded the circumstance, and added that I felt much interested in proving whether the subject of my dream would still be faithful to me, travel-tired, and in that remote place. No. I lost the beloved figure of my vision in parting with the secret. My sleep has never looked upon it since, in sixteen years, but once. I was in Italy, and awoke (or seemed to awake), the well-remembered voice distinctly in my ears, conversing with it. I entreated it, as it rose above my bed and soared up to the vaulted roof of the old room, to answer me a question I had asked touching the future life. My hands were still outstretched towards it as it vanished, when I heard a bell ringing by the garden wall, and a voice in the deep stillness of the night calling on all good Christians to pray for the souls of the dead.[107]

Lord, you know how we contemplate thoughts of 'the future life' – that which is yet to come. We wonder what it might be like, and whom we might meet in the 'world of shadows' that is yet a distant prospect. However we each choose to commemorate the memory of our dear departed, with flowers, prayers, the lighting of candles, or in other ways, I pray your blessing upon all such anniversaries. No-one has any monopoly on how such commemorations should take place. Some 'pray for the souls of the dead' and find comfort in doing so, while others prefer different avenues of memory. In all your tenderness, Lord, comfort those who look to carry on after the loss of a loved one, and for whom this will be a different kind of Christmas.

Sacred infant, all divine,
What a tender love was thine,
Thus to come from highest bliss
Down to such a world as this.[108]

---

[107]   *The Holly Tree.*
[108]   From the carol *See amid the winter's snow.*

**Sovereign Lord, as you have promised, you may now dismiss your servant in peace.
(Luke 2:29 NIV)**

Our sufferings from cold and wet were far greater than our sufferings from hunger. We managed to keep the child warm, but I doubt if anyone else among us was ever warm for five minutes altogether; and the shivering, and the chattering of teeth, were sad to hear . . . Mrs. Atherfield, in getting little Lucy to sleep, sang her a song. She had a soft, melodious voice, and, when she had finished it, our people looked up and begged for another. She sang them another, and after it had fallen dark ended with the Evening Hymn. From that time, whenever anything could be heard above the sea and wind, and while she had any voice left, nothing would serve the people but that she should sing at sunset. She always did, and always ended with the Evening Hymn. We mostly took up the last line, and shed tears when it was done, but not miserably. We had a prayer night and morning, also, when the weather allowed of it.[109]

I give thanks today, Lord, for those individuals, clergy or otherwise, who prepare and lead services of prayer within the Church, be they informal prayer meetings or fixed Daily Offices. What a beautiful thing a regular pattern of prayer can be; rich in meaning, routine and benefit. Thank you, Heavenly Father, for those within my own church who faithfully give of their time to facilitate and organise hours of prayer. This Christmas, I give thanks especially for those who will once

---

[109] *The Wreck of the Golden Mary.*

102

again diligently brave cold weather to make church buildings available for sacred devotional moments. Bless their special ministry.

❧ —— ❧

Give thanks to God always,
O thou man, O thou man,
Give thanks to God always,
With hearts most jolly:
Give thanks to God always
Upon this blessèd day;
Let all men sing and say.
Holy, holy.[110]

---

[110] From the carol *Remember*, or *Remember O thou man*, probably sixteenth century, by Thomas Ravenscroft (c.1588-1635), English musician, composer, theorist and editor.

**Carry each other's burdens, and in this way
you will fulfil the law of Christ.
(Galatians 6:2 NIV)**

Although I am an old man, night is generally my time for walking. In the summer I often leave home early in the morning, and roam about fields and lanes all day, or even escape for days or weeks together; but, saving in the country, I seldom go out until after dark, though, heaven be thanked, I love its light and feel the cheerfulness it sheds upon the earth, as much as any creature living. I have fallen insensibly into this habit, both because it favours my infirmity and because it affords me greater opportunity of speculating on the characters and occupations of those who fill the streets. The glare and hurry of broad noon are not adapted to idle pursuits like mine; a glimpse of passing faces caught by the light of a streetlamp or a shop window is often better for my purpose than their full revelation in the daylight; and, if I must add the truth, night is kinder in this respect than day . . . That constant pacing to and fro, that never-ending restlessness, that incessant tread of feet wearing the rough stones smooth and glossy; is it not a wonder how the dwellers in narrows ways can bear to hear it! Think of a sick man in such a place as Saint Martin's Court, listening to the footsteps, and in the midst of pain and weariness obliged, despite himself (as though it were a task he must perform), to detect the child's step from the man's, the slipshod beggar from the booted exquisite, the lounging from the busy, the dull heel of the sauntering outcast from the quick tread of an expectant pleasure-seeker: think of the hum and noise always being present to his sense, and of the stream of life that will not stop, pouring on, on, on, through all his restless dreams, as if he were condemned to lie, dead but conscious, in a noisy churchyard, and had no hope of rest for centuries to come. Then, the crowds forever passing and repassing on the bridges (on those which are free of toll at least), where many stop on fine evenings looking listlessly down upon the water with some vague idea that by and by it runs between green banks which grow wider and wider until at last it joins the broad vast sea, where some halt to rest from heavy loads and think as they look over the parapet that to smoke and lounge away one's life, and lie sleeping in the sun upon a hot tarpaulin, in a dull, slow, sluggish barge, must be happiness unalloyed.[111]

Christmas crowds jostle, Lord, as last-minute shoppers hustle and bustle their way in and out of shops. Shop windows illuminate the scene, as buses and trains carry present-buyers and their purchases to and fro. And, yet, Lord, I know nothing of the burdens that are also carried: the recently bereaved, trying valiantly to keep going, the lonely, buying Christmas dinners for one, those who are plunging ever-deeper into debt with everything they buy, to keep up appearances, the shop worker at the end of their tether. Remind me, Lord, to be kind as I too make my way around, patient if I need to queue, and considerate in a way that might make all the difference to someone else.

Sire, the night is darker now, and the wind blows stronger: Fails my heart, I know not how: I can go no longer.'
'Mark my footsteps, good my page: tread thou in them boldly: Thou shalt find the winter's rage freeze thy blood less coldly.'[112]

---

[111] *The Old Curiosity Shop.*
[112] From *Good King Wenceslas* by J. M. Neale.

Uphold the cause of the poor and the oppressed.
(Psalm 82:3 NIV)

I entertain a weak idea that the English people are as hard-worked as any people upon whom the sun shines. I acknowledge to this ridiculous idiosyncrasy, as a reason why I would give them a little more play. In the hardest working part of Coketown; in the innermost fortifications of that ugly citadel, where Nature was as strongly bricked out as killing airs and gases were bricked in; at the heart of the labyrinth of narrow courts upon courts, and close streets upon streets, which had come into existence piecemeal, every piece in a violent hurry for some one man's purpose, and the whole an unnatural family, shouldering, and trampling, and pressing one another to death; in the last close nook of this great exhausted receiver, where the chimneys, for want of air to make a draught, were built in an immense variety of stunted and crooked shapes, as though every house put out a sign of the kind of people who might be expected to be born in it; among the multitude of Coketown, generically called 'the Hands,' a race who would have found more favour with some people, if Providence had seen fit to make them only hands, or, like the lower creatures of the seashore, only hands and stomachs, lived a certain Stephen Blackpool, forty years of age. Stephen looked older, but he had had a hard life. It is said that every life has its roses and thorns; there seemed, however, to have been a misadventure or mistake in Stephen's case, whereby somebody else had become possessed of his roses, and he had become possessed of the same somebody else's thorns in addition to his own. He had known, to use his words, a peck of trouble. He was usually called Old Stephen, in a kind of rough homage to the fact. A rather stooping man, with a knitted brow, a pondering expression of face, and a hard-looking head sufficiently capacious, on which his iron-grey hair lay long and thin, Old Stephen might have passed for a particularly intelligent man in his condition. Yet he was not. He took no place among those remarkable 'Hands,' who, piecing together their broken intervals of leisure through many years, had mastered difficult sciences, and acquired a knowledge of most unlikely things. He held no station among the Hands who could make speeches and carry on debates. Thousands of his compeers could talk much better than he, at any time. He was a good power-loom weaver, and a man of perfect integrity.[113]

This Christmas-time, Lord, when materialism is to the fore, help me to remember those trapped in modern-day slave labour, and to tailor my purchases accordingly. Grant me the presence of mind to check out ethical supply routes and options before I arrive at the checkout. I pray your blessing, God of justice, upon individuals, churches, and organisations seeking to defend the rights of the poor and the exploited, and champion their cause.

Where is the golden cradle
That Christ was rockèd in?
Where are the silken sheets
That Jesus was wrapt in?[114]

---

[113] *Hard Times.*
[114] From *The carnal and the crane*, an ancient ballad depicting a conversation between two birds who were discussing the birth of Christ. It is not known exactly what type of bird a carnal might have been.

**Jesus Christ is the same yesterday and today and forever.
(Hebrews 13:8 NIV)**

It was a hard frost, that day. The air was bracing, crisp, and clear. The wintry sun, though powerless for warmth, looked brightly down upon the ice it was too weak to melt, and set a radiant glory there ... The year was old, that day. The patient year had lived through the reproaches and misuses of its slanderers, and faithfully performed its work. Spring, summer, autumn, winter. It had laboured through the destined round, and now laid down its weary head to die. Shut out from hope, high impulse, active happiness, itself, but active messenger of many joys to others, it made appeal in its decline to have its toiling days and patient hours remembered, and to die in peace . . . The streets were full of motion, and the shops were decked out gaily. The New Year, like an infant heir to the whole world, was waited for, with welcomes, presents, and rejoicings. There were books and toys for the New Year, glittering trinkets for the New Year, dresses for the New Year, schemes of fortune for the New Year; new inventions to beguile it . . . The New Year, the New Year. Everywhere the New Year! The old year was already looked upon as dead; and its effects were selling cheap, like some drowned mariner's aboard ship. Its patterns were last year's, and going at a sacrifice, before its breath was gone. Its treasures were mere dirt, beside the riches of its unborn successor![115]

Out with the old and in with the new, Lord? In terms of annual traditions, customs, diaries, and calendars, yes, of course, but in terms of your unchanging love? Certainly not. As this year reaches

[115]   *The Chimes.*

108

its conclusion and gives way to its yet 'unborn successor,' I thank you, Lord Jesus, that your covenanted mercy remains the same. Changes come and changes go, but your nature, your goodwill, and your reliability do not alter in any way at all. Help me, I pray, to lean upon that eternal truth with the whole weight of faith, so that, whatever else may be lost or replaced, and however many years may pass, my heart may relax in the permanency of your grace.

Here we bring new water
From the well so clear,
For to worship God with,
This happy New Year.[116]

---

[116] From an old Welsh folk song, *Levy-Dew*, or *A New Year carol*, that has, over centuries, included lyrics written by several different people.

Mary the mother of Jesus.
(Acts 1:14 NIV)

The wine merchant sat in his dining room next morning, to receive the personal applicants for the vacant post in his establishment. It was an old-fashioned wainscoted room; the panels ornamented with festoons of flowers carved in wood; with an oaken floor, a well-worn Turkey carpet, and dark mahogany furniture . . . Such a Columbus of a morning was the summer morning, that it discovered Cripple Corner. The light and warmth pierced in at the open windows, and irradiated the picture of a lady hanging over the chimney-piece, the only other decoration of the walls. 'My mother at five-and-twenty,' said Mr. Wilding to himself, as his eyes enthusiastically followed the light to the portrait's face, 'I hang up here, in order that visitors may admire my mother in the bloom of her youth and beauty. My mother at fifty I hang in the seclusion of my own chamber, as a remembrance sacred to me. O! It's you, Jarvis!' These latter words he addressed to a clerk who had tapped at the door, and now looked in. 'Yes, sir. I merely wished to mention that it's gone ten, sir, and that there are several females in the counting-house.' 'Dear me!' said the wine-merchant, deepening in the pink of his complexion and whitening in the white, 'are there several? So many as several? I had better begin before there are more. I'll see them one by one, Jarvis, in the order of their arrival.'[117]

Lord Jesus, I do not presume to know much about your childhood, your upbringing, your family concerns. What comes

[117]   *No Thoroughfare.*

to mind here, though, is the crucial role your mother played in your life; from birth in Bethlehem to the gradual revelation of you, her physical, biological son, as the Saviour of the world. She was certainly no ordinary mother, Lord, and hers was a unique calling: truly, a landmark in history; one unusually full of emotion, love, and spiritual depth. I give thanks for your mother today, Lord, and for her pivotal obedience in helping to usher in the day of salvation; allowing herself to be bathed in the light of heaven before she bathed you as her baby boy. Thank you, God, for Mary.

The angel Gabriel from heaven came,
His wings as drifted snow, his eyes as flame;
'All hail,' said he, 'O lowly maiden Mary.'
Most highly favoured lady, Gloria!
'For know a blessèd mother you shall be,
All generations praise continually,
Your Son shall be Emmanuel, by seers foretold.'
Most highly favoured lady, Gloria![118]

[118]   Traditional Basque carol, translated and paraphrased by Sabin Baring-Gould.

111

Philip found Nathanael and told him, 'We have found the
one Moses wrote about in the Law, and about whom the
prophets also wrote – Jesus of Nazareth, the son
of Joseph.' 'Nazareth! Can anything good come
from there?' Nathanael asked.
(John 1:45, 46 NIV)

When Our Missis went away upon her journey, Mrs. Sniff
was left in charge. She did hold the public in check
most beautiful! In all my time, I never see half so many cups
of tea given without milk to people as wanted it with, nor half
so many cups of tea with milk given to people as wanted it
without. When foaming ensued, Mrs. Sniff would say: 'Then
you'd better settle it among yourselves, and change with one
another.' It was a most highly delicious lark . . . Our Missis
returned. It got circulated among the young ladies, and it
as it might be penetrated to me through the crevices of the
Bandolining Room, that she had Orrors to reveal, if revelations
so contemptible could be dignified with the name. Agitation
become awakened. Excitement was up in the stirrups.
Expectation stood a-tiptoe. At length it was put forth that on
our slacked evening in the week, and at our slackest time of
that evening betwixt trains, Our Missis would give her views
of foreign refreshmenting, in the Bandolining Room. It was
arranged tasteful for the purpose. The Bandolining table and
glass was hid in a corner, a arm-chair was elevated on a packing-
case for Our Missis's ockypation, a table and a tumbler of water
(no sherry in it, thankee) was placed beside it . . . The whole had
a beautiful appearance, with which the beauty of the sentiments
corresponded. On Our Missis's brow was wrote Severity, as she
ascended the fatal platform. (Not that that was anythink new.)

Miss Whiff and Miss Piff sat at her feet. Three chairs from the Waiting Room might have been perceived by a average eye, in front of her, on which the pupils was accommodated. Behind them a very close observer might have discerned a Boy. Myself. 'Where,' said Our Missis, glancing gloomily around, 'is Sniff?' 'I thought it better,' answered Mrs. Sniff, 'that he should not be let to come in. He is such an ass.' 'No doubt,' assented Our Missis. 'But for that reason is it not desirable to improve his mind?' 'Oh, nothing will ever improve HIM,' said Mrs. Sniff.[119]

Thank you, Lord Jesus, that an immense amount of good did indeed come from Nazareth!

Though poor be the chamber,
Come here, come and adore;
Lo! the Lord of heaven
Hath to mortals given
Life forevermore.[120]

[119] *Mugby Junction. Mugby Junction* is a set of short stories written in by Charles Dickens and collaborators Charles Collins, Amelia B. Edwards, Andrew Halliday, and Hesba Stretton. It was first published in a Christmas edition of the magazine *All the Year Round*. Dickens penned most of the issue.
[120] From the carol *Nazareth* by Henry Fothergill (1808-1872), a member of staff at the London Athenaeum who published novels and several songs.

Honor the LORD with your wealth.
(Proverbs 3:9 NIV)

'When a man at five-and-twenty can put his hat on, and can say 'this hat covers the owner of this property and of the business which is transacted on this property,' I consider, Mr. Bintrey, that, without being boastful, he may be allowed to be deeply thankful. I don't know how it may appear to you, but so it appears to me.' Thus Mr. Walter Wilding to his man of law, in his own counting-house; taking his hat down from its peg to suit the action to the word, and hanging it up again when he had done so, not to overstep the modesty of nature. An innocent, open-speaking, unused-looking man, Mr. Walter Wilding, with a remarkably pink and white complexion, and a figure much too bulky for so young a man, though of a good stature. With crispy curling brown hair, and amiable bright blue eyes. An extremely communicative man: a man with whom loquacity was the irrestrainable outpouring of contentment and gratitude. Mr. Bintrey, on the other hand, a cautious man, with twinkling beads of eyes in a large overhanging bald head, who inwardly but intensely enjoyed the comicality of openness of speech, or hand, or heart. 'Yes,' said Mr. Bintrey. 'Yes. Ha, ha!' A decanter, two wine glasses, and a plate of biscuits, stood on the desk. 'You like this forty-five-year-old port-wine?' said Mr. Wilding. 'Like it?' repeated Mr. Bintrey. 'Rather, Sir!' 'It's from the best corner of our best forty-five-year-old bin,' said Mr. Wilding. 'Thank you, sir,' said Mr. Bintrey. 'It's most excellent.'[121]

I suppose, Lord, it's only natural, at this time of year, to reflect, to take stock, and to look ahead to a new, approaching season of work and (possibly) commercial success. Likewise, we might

[121]   *No Thoroughfare.*

want to survey, with sincere gratitude and appreciation, any particularly pleasing Christmas presents we have received. We might also care to offer hospitality with the hope of impressing visitors with tangible tokens of prosperity. All well and good, so far as these things go, as long as we are mindful to remember that not everyone is similarly blessed. Help us, then, Lord, to enjoy our successes and achievements, with sincere thanksgiving, but never to the detriment or neglect of others, who might not be so fortunate. Grant us a spirit of gratitude mingled with sensitivity, humility, and an awareness of those around us and their situations.

On the first day of Christmas my true love sent to me . . . [122]

[122]   From the ballad *The twelve days of Christmas*, first published in 1780 (authorship uncertain). Subsequent versions have appeared since.

When they saw the star, they were overjoyed.
(Matthew 2:10 NIV)

'I will live in the past, the present, and the future!' Scrooge repeated, as he scrambled out of bed. 'The spirits of all three shall strive within me. Oh Jacob Marley! Heaven, and the Christmas-time be praised for this! I say it on my knees, old Jacob; on my knees!' He was so fluttered and so glowing with his good intentions, that his broken voice would scarcely answer to his call. He had been sobbing violently in his conflict with the Spirit, and his face was wet with tears. 'They are not torn down,' cried Scrooge, folding one of his bed-curtains in his arms, 'they are not torn down, rings and all. They are here, I am here, the shadows of the things that would have been, may be dispelled. They will be. I know they will!' His hands were busy with his garments all this time; turning them inside out, putting them on upside down, tearing them, mislaying them, making them parties to every kind of extravagance. 'I don't know what to do!' cried Scrooge, laughing and crying in the same breath . . . 'I am as light as a feather, I am as happy as an angel, I am as merry as a schoolboy. I am as giddy as a drunken man. A merry Christmas to everybody! A happy New Year to all the world. Hallo here! Whoop! Hallo!' He had frisked into the sitting-room, and was now standing there: perfectly winded.

'There's the saucepan that the gruel was in!' cried Scrooge, starting off again, and going round the fireplace. 'There's the door, by which the Ghost of Jacob Marley entered! There's the corner where the Ghost of Christmas Present, sat! There's the window where I saw the wandering spirits! It's all right, it's all true, it all happened. Ha ha ha!' Really, for a man who had been out of practice for so many years, it was a splendid laugh, a most

illustrious laugh. The father of a long, long line of brilliant laughs!
. . . He was checked in his transports by the churches ringing out
the lustiest peals he had ever heard. Clash, clang, hammer; ding,
dong, bell. Bell, dong, ding; hammer, clang, clash! Oh, glorious,
glorious! Running to the window, he opened it, and put out his
head. No fog, no mist; clear, bright, jovial, stirring, cold; cold,
piping for the blood to dance to; golden sunlight; heavenly sky;
sweet fresh air; merry bells. Oh, glorious! Glorious![123]

'On my knees!'

*Lord Jesus, may this season find us on our knees;
metaphorically, literally, or both, in celebration, worship and
adoration.*

'A happy New Year to all the world.'

*Lord Jesus, may this season inspire within us a spirit of
charity and goodwill; one that captures and reflects the essence of
these days.*

'The churches ringing out the lustiest peals.'

*Lord Jesus, bless your Church throughout this busy season,
as all kinds of endeavours are planned, in terms of social care and
outreach.*

Hark how the bells, sweet silver bells
All seem to say 'throw cares away!'
Christmas is here, bringing good cheer
To young and old, meek and the bold.[124]

123   *A Christmas Carol.*
124   An adaptation of the Ukrainian New Year's bell carol *Shchedryk.*

**Wake up, sleeper, rise . . . and Christ will shine on you.
(Ephesians 5:15 NIV)**

[Scrooge] was early at the office next morning. Oh, he was early there. If he could only be there first, and catch Bob Cratchit coming late! That was the thing he had set his heart upon. And he did it; yes, he did! The clock struck nine. No Bob. A quarter past. No Bob. He was full eighteen minutes and a half behind his time. Scrooge sat with his door wide open, that he might see him come into the tank. His hat was off, before he opened the door; his comforter too. He was on his stool in a jiffy; driving away with his pen, as if he were trying to overtake nine o'clock. 'Hallo!' growled Scrooge, in his accustomed voice, as near as he could feign it. 'What do you mean by coming here at this time of day?' 'I am very sorry, sir,' said Bob. 'I *am* behind my time.' 'You are?' repeated Scrooge. 'Yes. I think you are. Step this way, sir, if you please.' 'It's only once a year, sir,' pleaded Bob, appearing from the tank. 'It shall not be repeated. I was making rather merry yesterday, sir.' 'Now, I'll tell you what, my friend,' said Scrooge, 'I am not going to stand this sort of thing any longer. And therefore,' he continued, leaping from his stool, and giving Bob such a dig in the waistcoat that he staggered back into the tank again; 'and therefore I am about to raise your salary!' Bob trembled, and got a little nearer to the ruler. He had a momentary idea of knocking Scrooge down with it, holding him, and calling to the people in the court for help and a strait-waistcoat. 'A merry Christmas, Bob!' said Scrooge, with an earnestness that could not be mistaken, as he clapped him on the back. 'A merrier Christmas, Bob, my good fellow, than I have given you, for many a year! I'll raise your salary, and endeavour to assist your struggling family, and we will discuss your affairs this very afternoon, over a Christmas bowl of smoking bishop,[125] Bob! Make up the fires, and buy another coal-scuttle before you dot another i, Bob Cratchit!'[126]

———————

A season of reconciliation, repentance, and renewal: may that lovely trio of Christmas gems shine brightly in my life at this time of year, Lord Jesus.

———————

Christians, awake! Salute the happy morn
On which the saviour of the world was born;
Rise to adore the mystery of love
Which hosts of angels chanted from above!
With them the joyful tidings first begun
of God incarnate and the Virgin's Son.[127]

[125]   A type of mulled wine.
[126]   *A Christmas Carol.*
[127]   From the carol of the same name by John Byrom (1691 or 1692-1763), inventor of a revolutionary system of shorthand, landowner, and poet.